Texas Graveyards

Number Thirteen   The Elma Dill Russell Spencer Foundation Series

Texas Graveyards

A CULTURAL LEGACY   by Terry G. Jordan

UNIVERSITY OF TEXAS PRESS

Third Paperback Printing, 1990

Requests for permission to reproduce material from
this work should be sent to Permissions, University
of Texas Press, Box 7819, Austin, Texas 78713-7819.

∞ The paper used in this publication meets the
minimum requirements of American National
Standard for Information Sciences—Permanence
of Paper for Printed Library Materials, ANSI
Z39.48-1984.

Library of Congress Cataloging in Publication Data
Jordan, Terry G.
    Texas graveyards.
    Bibliography: p.
    Includes index.
    1. Cemeteries—Texas.   2. Sepulchral
monuments—Texas.   3. Texas—Social life and
customs.   I. Title.
GT3210.T4J67   393'.1'09764   81-14816
ISBN 0-292-78070-2 (pbk.)   AACR2

To the Old Ones

Contents

Acknowledgments

THE OBLIGATIONS that I have accumulated in the course of this study are numerous and diverse. For responding informatively to my questionnaires concerning graveyards in their areas, I am indebted to Peggy Tobin of Bandera, Mrs. Jack Hogg of Gilmer, Mrs. Tony H. Booth of Paris, Carolyn Ericson of Nacogdoches, Mrs. Howard W. Johnson of Valley Mills, and Vernon Schuder of Walker County. I enjoyed cemetery tramping in the learned company of Grady Shivers, Jr., of rural Beckville; Walter Freytag of La Grange; and Robert H. Almand of San Antonio. Mr. Almand was also kind enough to share with me his extensive knowledge and remarkable collection of tombstone photographs, accumulated over years of amateur cemetery research. Also sharing their expertise with me were Tom Harvey of Minneapolis; Donald B. Ball of Louisville; Jean Andrews Smith of Austin, the leading expert on Texas shells; Professor Solveig Olsen of North Texas State University, who provided a Norwegian translation; my father, Professor Gilbert J. Jordan of Dallas, who called my attention to the mention of hex signs in Goethe's *Faust*, assisted with several epitaph translations, and shared many a pleasurable cemetery tramp with me; Professor John M. Vlach of the University of Texas, an expert on Afro-American culture; Jerry Eidem; and Libby Marsh.

Photographs taken by Olin McCormick of Denton, John Henry Kothmann of Dallas, Anita Pitchford of Farmers Branch, and Francis E. Abernethy of Stephen F. Austin State University appear, with their kind permission, in this book. Similarly, several writers have generously allowed me to quote directly and abundantly from their scholarly works, for which I am most grateful. They include Sara Clark of Austin, Professor John R. Stilgoe of Harvard University, anthropologist Donald B. Ball, and Professor Fred B. Kniffen of Louisiana State University. I have also drawn extensively upon the research of my own students, in particular Martha Stone, Peter Kosinski, Theodore Albrecht, Anita Pitchford, Peggy G. Gough, Bill Whitehead, Marsha A. Keffer, Harry Disch, Charles L. Templeton, Lynette Schroeder, and Darla Allcorn.

On two different occasions, the Faculty Research Committee of North Texas State University provided generous financial assistance to me in this project. These were grant numbers 34315 (1974–1975) and 34288 (1977–1978).

Without the collective help of these diverse individuals, the study would scarcely have been possible, but any errors of fact or interpretation which might appear in this work are solely my responsibility.

Texas Graveyards

The Truth about Cemeteries

MY ATTRACTION to Texas cemeteries does not rest upon a fascination with death. I am not in the least thanatophilic and have instead long entertained, even nurtured, a healthy fear of death. Nor was I drawn to these landscapes of the dead, as so many are, by genealogy or the loss of loved ones. Death remained a stranger throughout my researches, never touching those close to me. Rather, my first visits to the cemeteries of Texas occurred as a result of a project I undertook to chart the spatial distribution of ethnic and cultural groups in the state, in particular the Germans (Fig. 1-1).[1] I compiled the resultant map, in no small part, from surname counts of tombstones in hundreds of rural and small-town graveyards across Texas. During these early years of cemetery tramping, I gradually became aware of four noteworthy truths about traditional burial grounds.

Necrogeography

First, and most important from my perspective as a cultural geographer, I learned that many characteristics of traditional Texas cemeteries differ greatly from one ethnic group to another, from one district to its neighbor. I found, for example, along the boundary between German-settled areas and neighboring regions occupied by southern Anglo-Americans, that more than mere surnames differed from one side to the other. Instead, the whole material culture of death clearly reflected the presence of the boundary. Soon I was able to distinguish German from Anglo

cemeteries even before I had approached near enough to read surnames or other inscriptions. And when, as often occurred, some Mexican graves were included in these dominantly Anglo and German cemeteries, I found that they, too, could easily be distinguished from a distance, their specific ethnicity revealed by rough wooden crosses and elaborate floral decoration.

Subsequent cemetery tramping in the Midwest, New England, and Europe reinforced my realization that major regional/ethnic variations existed in graveyard types; that a vivid "necrogeography," or regionality of burial practices, awaited description, classification, and analysis (Fig. 1-2).[2] Before I was finished with my ethnic map, I had become convinced that the traditional cemeteries of Texas provide one of the best indices to the cultural diversity of the state. Nowhere else, perhaps, is the imprint of Texas' multiple peopling still so sharp and clear as in the places we set aside for our dead (Fig. 1-3).

The Living and the Dead

The second truth about cemeteries may sound trite or even absurd. Graveyards, I learned, are not primarily for the dead, but for the living. My initial forays into rural cemeteries were clouded by a sense of guilt at disturbing the dead. I felt like an intruder and trespasser in an afterworld where I did not belong, and I hastily snatched the desired surnames before fleeing back to the domain of the living. Only gradually, through observa-

FIG. 1-1. A German Catholic tombstone, commemorating birth in Westphalia, stands in the St. Peter's Parish cemetery at Lindsay, Cooke County, Texas. Note also the graveyard crucifix. The epitaph reads "Katharina Hundt / Geb. / Juni 10. 1831 / Zu Attendorn Westfalen / Gest. / Jan. 20, 1917 / Zu Lindsay Cooke Co. Tex. / Herr, gib ihr die ewige / Ruhe und das ewige / Licht leuchte ihr" ["Katharina Hundt / Born / June 10, 1831 / At Attendorn, Westphalia / Died / Jan. 20, 1917 / At Lindsay Cooke Co., Tex. / Lord, give her eternal / rest and light the eternal / light for her"]. Photo by the author, 1973.

FIG. 1-2. A typical Louisiana French above-ground vault burial, New Orleans. Photo by the author, 1979.

LOUISIANA NECROGEOGRAPHY

"In Louisiana, with its sharp cultural divergence, the expected contrasts in burial practices appear. . . . French and Catholic south Louisiana has large central cemeteries composed of above-surface, white vaults on sanctified ground adjoining rural and small-town churches [see Fig. 1-2]. These practices have largely extended to smaller congregations of Anglo-Saxon Protestants, particularly Episcopalians, within the general area. The distinctive use of above-surface vaults has been ascribed to sanitary precautions during fever epidemics in New Orleans and to a humanistic reaction to a high water table. . . .

"Rural north Louisiana follows the practices common to the upland South. Interment is beneath the ground, with a general east-west orientation of the graves. Markers are usually plain, and contrast strikingly with those of south Louisiana in the absence of crosses. Isolated family cemeteries are probably prevalent numerically, the locations of abandoned and overgrown burial grounds identified by groves of planted cedar trees. Here and there clusters of small gabled roofs shelter individual graves. There are still annual 'scrapings,' when the grass is eradicated to leave the ground bare. Sea shells and bits of glass commonly border the grave plot."

—Fred Kniffen, "Necrogeography in the United States," p. 427. Reprinted with permission of the author and the American Geographical Society.

FIG. 1-3. The entrance to a Mexican American cemetery in Victoria County, Texas. Photo by the author, 1980.

LIFE IN A TENNESSEE GRAVEYARD

"The actual conduct of the day's activities gave more the impression of a homecoming or family reunion than of any event so solemn sounding as a 'Decoration Day.' Before lunch conversation groups tended to cluster in various family and age sets with discussions ranging from state politics to crops. The mid-day meal was provided by the women of each family bringing a basket lunch consisting of fried chicken, potato salad, bread, ice tea, [and] cold drinks . . . spread on a large, permanently installed, wooden table in one corner of the cemetery. . . . Lunch was served on paper plates and the low, flat gravestones served as convenient seats for youngsters and adults alike. Following lunch various conversational groups reconvened and an impromptu 'baseball' game was begun with several youngsters dashing across a number of graves chasing the ball."

> **—Donald B. Ball, "Social Activities Associated with Two Rural Cemeteries in Coffee County, Tennessee," pp. 95–96. Reprinted with permission from *Tennessee Folklore Society Bulletin.***

FIG. 1-4. Sign on the fence at Bethlehem Baptist Cemetery in the Blackland Prairie of Collin County. The local Hill Southern dialect, with its superabundant *r*'s, encouraged the writer to render "pecans" as "pircons." Sale of the pecans produced by the cemetery trees makes a substantial contribution to the maintenance fund. Photo by the author, 1980.

tion, did I come to regard the cemetery as a proper place for live people. Graveyards, after all, reflect the customs, beliefs, handicrafts, and social structure of the survivors.[3] At certain times of the year, such as "decoration day," they even provide the setting for valued, important social events.[4] One rural cemetery in Southeast Texas even has a "Welcome" sign attached to the fence. Indeed, painted messages to the living abound in Texas folk graveyards. "Your Donations Keep This Cemetery," proclaims a sign alongside the gate at rural Trinity Cemetery near Denton, and another communication in nearby Collin County establishes the graveyard's ownership of the pecans produced by trees within its bounds (Fig. 1-4). Visitors to Moss Hill Cemetery in Tyler County are advised that "All Graves Must Be Placed by the President—Law."[5] At aptly named Friendship Cemetery in Milam County, the startling presence of a rural mailbox atop a post in the burial ground is explained by a sign requesting that "visitors register here" (Fig. 1-5). Sure enough, a registry book and pencil are inside the mailbox. The Salado town cemetery offers a hand-powered pump, covered by a shed, to provide water for the thirsty visitor and the floral decorations (Fig. 1-6). Many graveyards, even those not adjacent to churches, have a board privy for the convenience of the temporary visitor.

The living, singly and in groups, are frequent visitors. They come to commune with the dead, to associate with friends and neighbors, to manicure and beautify the grounds, to record biographical data concerning their ancestors, to make rubbings of fine old tombstones, to vandalize and destroy, and even to study traditional material culture. In many Texas cemeteries, lawn chairs for visitors are placed alongside some graves (Fig. 1-7). Researchers in one Boston urban cemetery observed twenty-two categories of human activity, ranging from frisbee tossing, jogging, bicycling, and model airplane flying to berry picking, card playing, sleeping, playing hide-and-seek, and voyeurism. Even at that, the Boston researchers probably missed quite a few activities. If you wait and watch long

FIG. 1-5. Friendship Cemetery in Milam County requests guests, presumably the living, to sign in. Photo by the author, 1980.

FIG. 1-6. Water for the living, at the Salado town cemetery, Bell County. The metal shed was erected in 1954, but the pump is presumably much older. Photo by the author, 1980.

FIG. 1-7. Lawn furniture for the comfort of the visitor, Old Union Cemetery, Limestone County. Photo by the author, 1980.

enough, you will eventually witness living humankind display, in the graveyard, its gamut of behavior, from base to noble. I believe that cultural geographer Yi-fu Tuan erred in implying that cemeteries are "landscapes of fear." Clearly they are not—at least not during daylight hours.[6]

Too, I found that the rural folk do not distinguish so sharply between life and death as do we from the cities and universities. Death is, for them, intertwined so tightly with life as to be inseparable. They converse with the dead and leave favorite foods for the departed to consume. Life, death, and afterlife merge in the folk culture of the burial ground. The living have every right to be there.

Conservatism

A third truth concerning traditional Texas cemeteries was more difficult to perceive. After years of observing the highly diverse

material traits of southern, German, and Hispanic rural graveyards, I came to regard the traditional burial ground as an extremely conservative aspect of the respective cultures. Folkways survive better there than in the world at large. Perhaps rural cemeteries preserve archaic customs and practices better than do other facets of the culture because many people are superstitious about death and the dead. Time-tested techniques for laying the dead to rest and calming the spirits of the deceased tend to persist for centuries, even millennia, and the practitioners are reluctant to tamper with them. James Deetz, who knows well the rural graveyards of New England, reminds us that "religious institutions and their artifacts are known to be the most conservative aspects of a culture, resisting change."[7] He would likely also agree with me that cemeteries constitute the most conservative aspect of religious institutions. Geographer Fred Kniffen echoes these sentiments,

CHANGE COMES TO MOUNT PISGAH

"Notice: Centepede grass has been planted on grounds.
Do not cut or hoe from graves or grounds! Thank you."

—Sign posted in the Mount Pisgah Cemetery, Tyler County, Texas, 1975 (copied by Martha Stone).

noting that "since there is a special reluctance to disturb graveyards, they often lie surrounded by bustling urban activities, preserved for study longer than might normally be expected of an outmoded folkway."[8] Likewise, folklorist John M. Vlach concluded that, for black culture in America, the cemetery represents "the strongest material demonstration of African-inspired memories."[9]

In our rural burial grounds we find one of the last viable refuges of folk culture, with all the antiquity, timelessness, and continuity implied by that term. For, as John Stilgoe tells us, the traditional Christian graveyard is the work "of laymen seeking to objectify the most meaningful elements of a folk religion grounded in paganism."[10] Indeed, venerable practices, some of which long antedate Christianity, abound in many Texas cemeteries. Nowhere else, I maintain, is it possible to look so deeply into our people's past. No better place exists to ponder questions of culture

history and ancient ancestral cultural hearths. In more ways than one, we are closer to our forefathers when treading upon the ground where they lie buried.

Change

The fourth truth about rural and small-town graveyards may seem to contradict the third or, at the very least, to present a paradox. Change is occurring. In spite of the conservatism inherent in the cemetery institution and regardless of the native conservatism of most Texans—Anglo, black, Mexican, and German alike—the traditional graveyards are endangered. Few unaltered folk cemeteries survive in Texas; most burial grounds today reveal departures from the ancient, traditional material culture that prevailed a century ago. Rural depopulation, "perpetual care," and acculturation have already taken a heavy toll, and the rise of an all-pervading popular culture, represented by the modern commercial cemetery (the necrological equivalent of a fast-food joint), will likely obliterate most distinctive elements of the traditional Texas graveyards by the end of this century. In this sense, the cemetery can be regarded as a microcosm of southern folk culture. All traditions face an early demise, and landscapes of the past give way to cultural homogenization. Regionalism and provincialism fade; national culture ascends.

Folk burial practices are still to be seen, but generally the searcher must seek out remote graveyards in economically depressed districts to find the best surviving examples. Even there, the greatest rewards are found in the older sections of the cemeteries, away from mass-produced commercial tombstones and plastic flowers that speak of the twentieth century. Our present generation may be the last to have access to the incredibly rich material culture of the folk cemetery.

Two personal examples of this change illustrate what is happening: one from a rural Texas setting, the other from the suburbs of a great city. My maternal grandmother lies buried at Mount Zion Cemetery in rural Panola County, East Texas. She always believed, in common with the folk of the Deep South, that all grass should be hoed out of graveyards, leaving the bare earth exposed (Fig. 1-8). Grass growing on a grave was a sign of disrespect for the dead, she thought. Traditionally, Mount Zion reflected her belief and preference—grass was banished from its fenced enclosure. No doubt my grandmother expected that, when her time came to join the departed ancestors at Mount Zion, her grave would be similarly tended. Today, thirty years after her death, a lush green carpet of carefully manicured St. Augustine grass covers the entirety of Mount Zion, her grave included.

A mile or so from my boyhood home in North Dallas, atop a windy blackland prairie hill, a pioneer family, long before my time, established its private clan cemetery. In the early years, the small graveyard no doubt reflected the folk burial customs of Dallas County's farm people. By the 1940s, though, this simple graveyard had become the nucleus of one of Dallas' first commercial cemeteries, complete with mausoleum, funeral chapel, radio commercials, and professional gardeners. Folk and popular culture had clashed there amid the Johnson grass pastures on the northern outskirts of Dallas, with a predictable outcome.

FIG. 1-8. A traditional "scraped" southern folk cemetery, with all grass removed. The scene is in Shiloh Cemetery, near Bartonville in Denton County. Photo by the author, 1974.

Graveyard Scholars

Persuaded of these four truths—that traditional cemeteries in Texas displayed pronounced regional variation, a necrogeography offering a useful index to cultural identity and ethnicity; belonged properly to the domain of the living; preserved in refuge some truly venerable material culture, providing a potential key to antecedence and diffusion; and faced extinction in the immediate, foreseeable future—I began tarrying longer in these places, not merely recording the ethnic affiliation of the deceased but carefully noting, cataloging, and photographing the diverse, intriguing material culture. What appeared at first glance to be a chaotic, meaningless mixture of symbols and customs proved, upon close analysis, to contain fascinating clues to questions of cultural origins and spread. I redoubled my field research, acquired some modest funding to support my madness, delved deeply into libraries to discover what other scholars had learned from and about cemeteries, and sent some of the best among my students out to experience what I had and to help me learn.

I found, in the libraries, that I was by no means alone in my morbid interests. A great variety of scholars, among them archaeologists, anthropologists, folklorists, sociologists, and fellow cultural geographers, had preceded me. Prehistorians have long found graves and tombs rich sources of knowledge, though their practice of excavating and altering as they learned and preserved left me with a vaguely distressed feeling. Too, their interest was in long-dead cultures of the distant past, while mine concerned ways of life still extant, at least in vestige. From the archaeologist I could learn of the Classical Greek or prehistoric Celtic cemetery, but not much about the burial places of present-day rural Texans. True, some historical archaeologists have recently worked on grave sites in the American South, generally as part of the preparation of environmental impact statements, but their reports are as yet relatively few in number and difficult of access.[11]

Anthropologists have also traditionally viewed cemeteries as worthy of study. Physical anthropologists excavate graveyards in order to measure and classify the racial and skeletal characteristics of the deceased. Perusing their professional literature, I could learn, for example, that the Icelander's average height decreased steadily between about A.D. 1200 and 1800, coincident with a climatic deterioration in the North Atlantic. While worthy, their scholarly concerns were unrelated to mine. The cultural anthropologists, too, have been frequent visitors to folk cemeteries. Preponderantly, though, their research has been carried out in remote lands among non-Western peoples. From them I could find out much about the burial practices of African pygmies, Indochinese hill tribes, and Pacific islanders but relatively little about those of the present inhabitants of rural Texas.[12]

Sociologists have approached cemeteries asking questions relevant to their discipline, questions concerning the functioning of society, social status, and the symbolism that pervades human life. Material culture is not their domain or concern and, understandably, they devoted little attention to it. They did not have the answers I sought.

American folklorists, amateur and professional alike, I discovered, had devoted considerable study to the death lore of the American South and Mexico. Even so, their interests were still not precisely mine. Their attention usually focused on nonmaterial culture, on the lore surrounding death rather than the physical entity of the graveyard. They wrote of people who covered mirrors when death occurred, of ghosts lurking along the Cumberland and on the Brazos, of banning cats from rooms where corpses lay, of traditional funeral oratory.[13] But, with a few notable exceptions, they did not teach me about the material culture of the cemetery.[14]

Even journalists have occasionally visited and written about Texas cemeteries. They are usually attracted by strange or even bizarre elements of graveyard material culture—eye-grabbing features that testify to the general insanity of humankind. One of my students, ever seeking to please, once brought me such a newspaper clipping, now yellowed with age in my files. Regrettably, I cannot determine which paper or year it came from, since the student neatly scissored away the identifying dateline, frustrating my instinctual desire to footnote. In any case, the headline reads "Odd, Strange, and Curious," beneath which is a photograph of a massive tombstone shaped like a king-sized bed, complete with an imposing headboard and a two-poster footboard. "Man rests in peace in double bed," reads the caption, further explaining that the "unknown Texan wanted to take at least one of the comforts of home with him on his final journey." While individualism on this scale is commendable and perhaps reflective of Anglo-Texan idiosyncrasies, it tells me little about what is ordinary and typical of the folk culture. In my academic geographical training, I was taught to observe the commonplace and to ignore the freakish. Following journalists around, I concluded, was not going to teach me what I needed to know.

Instead, I found my true kindred spirits exactly where I should have expected them— among the small but hardy band of fellow cultural geographers. The seminal work was done by Fred Kniffen, the acknowledged founder and father figure of American folk-geography.[15] Kniffen's intellectual roots reached deep into the "Berkeley school" of cultural geography, developed by the late Carl O. Sauer at the University of California in the 1920s and 1930s.[16] In 1967, while I was still snatching surnames, Professor Kniffen published a stimulating call for research on traditional cemeteries, pointing out the great potential value of such studies.[17] "Formal disposal of the deceased," he wrote, "is a universal practice" and "should be an essential consideration in individual or comparative study" of the human occupance pattern. The cemetery "reflects traditional values, religious tenets, legal regulation, economic and social status, and even natural environment. Evolution, invention, and diffusion are as nicely exemplified here as with any other cultural phenomenon." In sum, said Kniffen, "there can be few other subjects as untouched or as promising as the geographical study of burial practices."[18] A number of Kniffen's students have carried out research on traditional

cemeteries in the decade following his appeal for study.[19]

In the same year that Kniffen's article appeared—1967—another cultural geographer of the Berkeley persuasion, David E. Sopher, lent vitality, impetus, and respect to the geographical study of religious faith through the publication of the first book in the English language on this subject.[20] Sopher's *The Geography of Religions* was widely read and stimulated a great deal of discussion and research.[21] Seemingly deriving his inspiration from French geographer Pierre Deffontaines' "geography of the dead," Professor Sopher devoted a short section of his book to differing burial customs.[22] My own work clearly belongs in the tradition developed by Kniffen, Sopher, and their students. In a broader sense, it belongs in the growing interdisciplinary field of "folklife" studies, in which cultural geographers play a major role.[23]

The Present Volume

In all, my cemetery tramping has occupied the better part of twenty years, the latter decade of which involved a systematic study of traditional material culture. During that period, only my closest friends, next-of-kin relatives, and most devoted students, if anyone, retained full confidence in my sanity and well-being, but then cultural geographers are by nature eccentric. From time to time in that latter decade, I read papers at professional meetings and published the tentative findings of my research, seeking advice, criticism, and encouragement from my peers.[24]

The present book is the culmination of my lengthy research. It deals with three distinct Texan geographies of death: southern, Hispanic-American, and German. These three represent, respectively, the numerically and spatially dominant host culture and two major ethnic minorities in the state. The southern folk cemetery tradition crosses racial lines to be shared by blacks, southern Anglo-Americans, and Alabama-Coushatta Indians. As such, it embodies the ancestral burial customs of well over half of the rural Texas population and is clearly the prevalent traditional type in the state. I have, accordingly, devoted two chapters to the southern graveyard. With southern whites and blacks joined in a single cemetery culture, a fitting union since their dead cohabit many an East Texas burial ground, the Hispanic and German traditions represent the next two largest population groups in the state. One chapter is devoted to each of these two major ethnic minorities.

By omitting consideration of the numerically lesser ethnic groups, I do not mean to imply that they lack worthy and distinctive cemetery traditions. Czechs, Norwegians, Cajun French, Poles, Jews, and Swedes, among others, practiced their own venerable burial customs (Fig. 1-9). Viewing a remarkable 1854 Gothic folk tombstone in the Norse cemetery in Bosque County, for example, can conjure up images of newly Christianized Vikings dwelling along the fjords of Norway (Fig. 1-10). Rather, my omission of these smaller minorities reflects the shallow depth of my own knowledge concerning their cultures and my inability to read their ancestral languages. Perhaps my book will stimulate better qualified persons to investigate and record the morbid material legacy of these numerous smaller groups. In the meantime, I content myself with a simple thanatological trisecting of Texas. Since the southern folk cemetery is the prevalent traditional type, I will begin with it.

FIG. 1-9. Jewish Hebrew tombstone in Shearith Israel Cemetery, Dallas. The burial practices and funerary symbolism of conservative Jews remain quite distinctive, even in an urban setting. Photo by the author, 1979.

FIG. 1-10. The oldest tombstone in the Norwegian Lutheran Cemetery at Norse, in Bosque County. Note the pointed Gothic shape of the stone and the St. Andrew's Cross. The lichen-splotched epitaph reads "Her hviler Anders Arnesen Braetta dod i 1854" ["Here rests Anders Arnesen Braetta died in 1854"]. Photo by the author, 1973.

The Southern
Folk Cemetery in Texas

AN UNINITIATED VISITOR in a traditional rural southern Protestant church and its nearby cemetery in eastern or central Texas might well be puzzled and astounded. In the plain white board chapel, the theology of Calvin, Wesley, and Knox discourages visual religious symbolism of almost every kind, even a simple cross and steeple.[1] Unless a painted sign identifies the chapel, the visitor will have difficulty ascertaining whether the structure is a house of worship, a school, or a lodge hall, so completely has the religious symbolism been rooted out. But beyond the arched gateway in the adjacent graveyard, a bewildering variety of symbols, largely pagan, compete for visual attention. The symbolism suppressed for centuries in the chapels seems to burst forth all the more vigorously in the cemetery, making the folk graveyard of eastern Texas and the American South a confusing, fascinating, and ultimately revealing place. Like so much of southern culture, the practices relating to burial cross racial lines. The folk cemetery of the South is characteristic of whites, blacks, and Indians alike; you will find it among the descendants of wealthy planters, "crackers," slaves, and southeastern Indian tribes.[2]

The first glimpse of such a cemetery truly startles the unsuspecting visitor (Fig. 2-1). Throughout the burial ground, the natural cover of grasses and weeds has been laboriously chopped or "scraped" away, revealing an expanse of red-orange East Texas soil or somber black prairie earth, sometimes deco-

rated with raked patterns. At each grave, this dirt is heaped in an elongated mound, oriented on an east-west axis and anchored by a head and foot stone. Upon the mound is deposited a remarkable variety of objects: shells, pieces of glass and pottery, toys, broken lamps, light bulbs, small decorated Christmas trees, razors, chunks of petrified wood, vases of flowers, snuff or medicine bottles, and similar items.[3] Additional visual relief is provided by a scattering of cedar or juniper evergreens; by rosebushes blooming along the surrounding fence; by iris, lilies, crape myrtles, gardenias, nandinas, and perhaps a holly or a yew.

Closer inspection reveals that burials are grouped by family, with rows of bricks, low fences, or curbs bounding the individual clan territories. Husbands lie to the south, or right, of their wives. An occasional grave or two may be covered by small, open-sided, roofed sheds. Tombstones are modest in size and inscribed with scant biographical information. A terse epitaph and an image of a dove or a lamb may also appear on the stone, though the Christian cross is absent here, as in the chapel. Under shade trees next to the burial ground, the visitor may spy long board serving tables or perhaps an open-sided tabernacle.

As often as not, no church or chapel stands alongside these cemeteries, and even if one is present, its founding normally postdates that of the burial ground. Clearly, the southern folk cemeteries are not sanctified ground. Many are located on private family property.

How are we to interpret the obvious dichotomy of chapel and graveyard? What can be the meaning of the curious, diverse material culture in the cemetery, of the rampant graveyard symbolism? Do the various artifacts, plants, and images bear a meaningful symbolic message that might profitably be deciphered by the student of Texas folklife? Twenty years of cemetery tramping and archival reading convince me that the answer is a resounding "yes."

I believe the southern folk cemetery to be a cultural conglomerate, containing contributions from each of the three main cultures—African, Amerindian, and European—responsible for the development of southern society and folkways. As such, it could provide an index for assessing the importance of the respective cultural contributions of these three groups, an index made all the more valuable because truly venerable customs have survived in the graveyards. Ancient, deposed deities banned from the chapel still lurk in the burial ground. In short, the graveyard may well be the best place in the American South to learn about and puzzle over cultural origins and diffusion.

Scraping

Perhaps no feature of the southern folk cemetery begs more for interpretation than the practice of scraping (Fig. 2-2). I have at several "workings" asked men who were laboriously chopping out grass and weeds from their family plots why they did so (Fig. 2-3). Most paused, leaned on their hoes, and appeared to consider the question for the first time in their lives. Some opined that it was "customary" or "looks nice" and a few saw it as a practical way to eliminate mowing, seemingly oblivious to the fact that scraping was a lot more work. My own grandmother, a woman with ancestral roots in Alabama and the Carolinas, merely declared that grass on a grave was "disrespectful to the dead." Folklorist Fred Tarpley got a similar answer when he asked the same question in Northeast Texas:

"Grandpaw killed himself keeping the weeds out of his cotton, and we're not about to let them grow on his grave now."[4] Obviously, the interview method was not going to provide the answers. The origin of scraping and most other practices related to the traditional southern cemetery was much too ancient to remain in the memory of present-day practitioners. The reasons had been forgotten countless generations ago in faraway lands.

Archival evidence was more helpful. It pointed to Africa as the likely source of graveyard scraping. Near equivalents to bare-earth cemeteries can be found in the traditional practices of the West African slave coast (Table 2-1). In northern Nigeria, for example, graves were covered with a mud plaster, and the Talense of the Ashanti hinterland in Ghana erected conical mud mounds over their graves.[5] Many tribes of that area made burials "in the earthen floor of the house," in swept-earth yards, or in regularly tilled gardens.[6] In each of these cases, bare earth lay atop the grave. I believe the scraped earth cemetery is an Africanism and goes hand-in-hand with the typically southern and African swept-earth yard surrounding dwellings. Indeed, southern folk typically refer in conversation to their cemeteries as "yards." Grass, in Africa and the South, was an unwelcomed intruder. Respectable people kept it chopped out of yards, fields, and burial grounds. Some rural Anglos in Texas even refer to scraping as "plowing." The ultimate African reasons were possibly the danger posed by grassfires and the proverbial snake in the grass. Removal of grass also kept loose livestock from grazing (and defecating) in yards and cemeteries. Or perhaps scraping came south across Africa to the slave coast long ago with Islam. In that case, the laboriously scraped Texas graveyard could be an effort to re-create, in a humid climate, the long-forgotten desert desolation of the Sahara and Arabia, where Moslem dead lie beneath the bare sand (see Fig. 2-4).

An African origin of cemetery scraping is further suggested by the distribution of this custom in America. Rarely does one encounter scraping outside the Gulf and South At-

FIG. 2-1. A scraped, mounded Anglo churchyard in rural Denton County. Adjacent to Trinity Church, this cemetery is still maintained in the traditional way. Photo by the author, 1974.

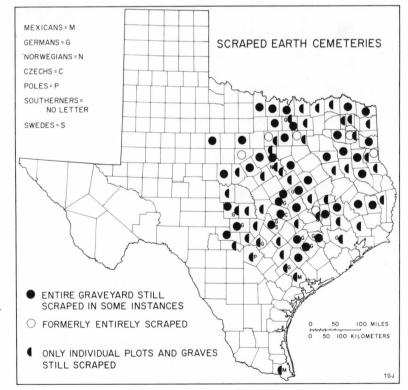

FIG. 2-2. Each symbol represents a county, but not all counties have been studied. Sources: field research; Schroeder, "Upland Southern Burial Traditions"; Stone, "Cemeteries in Tyler County"; Gough, "Cemetery Tradition in Tarrant County"; communications from Vernon Schuder, Eugene George, Mrs. Tony H. Booth, Mrs. Jack Hogg, and Carolyn Ericson.

FIG. 2-3. On "decoration day," a descendant of Tennessean immigrants works his scraped-earth family plot in Good Hope Cemetery, in the Blackland Prairie of Denton County. The graves in the foreground are Southern Baptist, those in the background Presbyterian. Photo by the author, 1974.

lantic coastal plains, the stronghold of rural blacks. The custom is apparently unknown or very rare in the hills of western North Carolina and in Middle Tennessee.[7] In Texas, scraping and swept-earth yards are found among southern Anglos, blacks, and the Alabama-Coushatta Indians. The custom is rapidly dying out, and relatively few cemeteries are completely scraped today. For example, in Tyler County only three of twenty-seven rural cemeteries inspected were fully scraped, but the majority revealed at least partial grass removal, while in Cass County none was fully scraped but three-quarters had some

bare-earth sections or plots.[8] Latter-day substitutes for scraping abound, including cement paving, graveling, and bricking of the plot.

Mounds and False Crypts

Traditionally, the scraped earth was heaped up in elongated mounds at each grave, giving the visual impression of fresh burial (Fig. 2-5). Seeing the grave mounds in a rural Alabama cemetery, a northern visitor wrote of "clay . . . raised in a long and narrow oval with a

Table 2-1. Origins of Southern Folk Cemetery Traits

	Pagan Mediterranean European	Pagan Northwestern European	Christian British European	Pagan African	Pagan Amerindian	American Frontier Innovations
Scraping of cemetery				x		
Mounding of graves		x		o	o	
Broken crockery on mound	o			x		
Lamps or light bulbs on mound	x					
Shells as decoration	o			x	o	
Rose bushes	x					
Cedar/juniper	o	x				
Flowers	x					
Burial with feet to east	o	o	x	o		
Burial of wrongdoers on north-south axis			x	o		
Wife buried to left of husband			x			
Family plots				o		x
Unsanctified ground			o	o		x
Tabernacle			o			x
Gravehouses				o	x	
Surrounding fence			x	o		
Lichgate			x			

x = likely origin   o = similar custom

sharp ridge, the shape exactly of an inverted boat." Pursuing his watery metaphors further, he saw the large assembly of such mounds as resembling "shoals of minnows."[9]

Mounding of graves was known to pre-Columbian Africans, Europeans, and Indians alike. Even into recent times, West African groups, such as the Dakahari of northern Nigeria, continue to "mark the grave by mounds."[10] A conical shape is perhaps most common for the African burial mounds, but elongated ones like those of the American South also occur, as among the Talense of Ghana and in Nubia (Fig. 2-4).[11] In the pre-Columbian American Southeast, some highly cultured Indian tribes built funerary mounds, but these were much more massive than the later Christian grave mounds and generally contained multiple burials. A more likely origin of the southern mounding custom is Britain. The antecedent is probably the "long barrow" grave, a pagan type dating back some three thousand years in the British Isles and later succeeded by the grass-covered, elongated mounds so typical of rural English churchyards still today.[12] But even if the custom is of British origin, it is significant that both blacks and the southeastern Indian

FIG. 2-4. Mounded, bare-earth graves marked by
head- and footstones, among the Nubian people of
the Sudan. This burial ground is strikingly like
those of the American South, suggesting an African
Muslim origin for some southern cemetery traits.
Each grave is covered with small rounded rocks, not
unlike the southern shell decoration custom. Photo
1963 by E. Ragazzini, ©WFP/Food and Agriculture
Organization of the United Nations, Rome, Italy;
used with permission.

tribes were culturally preconditioned by similar practices to accept grave mounding
(Table 2-1).

Less commonly, the traditional mound is
replaced by a low false crypt of brick, stone,
or concrete (Fig. 2-6). Though these structures
somewhat resemble the above-ground burials
of the Louisiana French, they actually cover
normal in-ground interments and are, in
effect, permanent mounds. Some false crypts,
according to Anita Pitchford, occur in almost
30 percent of all cemeteries in Cass County,
probably representative of East Texas.[13] I have
seen them in various other southern-populated
counties, always as a minority type. While
the temptation is strong to attribute false
crypts to Louisiana French influence, the fact
is they occur through much of the South. In
Muhlenberg County, Kentucky, for example,
many of the oldest interments are marked

FIG. 2-5. Mounded, bare-earth graves in the Alabama-Coushatta Indian reservation cemetery, Polk County, Texas. Note the rake pattern in the sand. This graveyard, though Amerindian, differs in no important respect from traditional white and black cemeteries in the same county. Photo by John Henry Kothmann, 1978; used with permission.

with vaultlike "box-grave covers" very similar to the Texas false crypts.[14] In South Carolina, tombs and false crypts dating from the colonial period occur in certain white cemeteries.

Grave Decoration

The bare-earth mounds provide a convenient surface upon which to place the incredible variety of items that typically appear atop graves in the South. For example, in the Alabama-Coushatta Indian cemetery in Polk County, I observed in 1969 on the grave mound of a recently deceased young man a pair of dark glasses, an empty bottle of aftershave lotion, a toy car, a safety razor, and a conch shell. In nearby Tyler County, a white child's grave mound served as a table for a miniature tea set. Some mounds bear a truly astounding array of material items (Fig. 2-7).

FIG. 2-6. Two false crypts of native hewn limestone
at the Salado town cemetery, Bell County. The
crypts, built in 1880 and 1887, cover normal in-
earth burials and occur as a minority type in many
southern folk cemeteries in Texas. Photo by the
author, 1980.

FIG. 2-7. Grave-mound decoration in this Bowie
County white cemetery includes toys, furniture,
and a great variety of vases with flowers. The
mounds had to be elongated to accommodate the
huge amount of decorative material. Photo by Olin
McCormick, 1979; used with permission.

Among these, broken crockery and pieces of glass provide the clearest examples of African influence.[15] In West and Central Africa, pottery was broken at the grave site, possibly to symbolize the shattered life, and the custom seems to have survived intact in America. According to one southern black, "you break the dishes so that the chain will be broke" and no other deaths will occur in the family.[16] The broken dishes, typically, are among the last objects used by the deceased immediately prior to death. Broken pottery is also occasionally associated with burial in southern Europe, as in pre-Christian Greece, but the custom does not seem to have survived into later times there.[17] The practice of diverse objects atop burials also has deep roots in the British Isles, particularly Ireland, where dishes, pipes, and stones are found as grave decoration.[18] The large Scotch-Irish element in southern white ancestry is likely partially responsible for the vigor of this custom in the South.

The appearance of lamps and even light bulbs on some southern grave mounds is tantalizingly similar to the practice, especially common among the ancient Greeks and Romans, of burying lamps with the dead to light their journey in the underworld.[19] In some parts of modern Europe, including Switzerland, lanterns are placed atop graves, a custom almost identical to that of the American South.[20] Also in both the South and the pagan Mediterranean, objects relating to the profession of the deceased were associated with burial.[21]

Bottles also find their way onto southern grave mounds. Among blacks, the bottles containing medicine used prior to death are often placed on the mound. Inverted snuff bottles are also a favorite grave decoration among Texas blacks and poor whites of the Lower South (Fig. 2-8).

Of the diverse objects on southern grave mounds, none is more intriguing or potentially informative than the shell (Fig. 2-9).[22] All across the Coastal Plain, from the Carolina Tidewater to Central Texas, shells adorn burials—seashells and freshwater shells: mussel, clam, cowrie, cockle, and conch

shells alike (Fig. 2-10). Inverted clam-type shells, boiled white, often cover entire grave mounds; sometimes single conches rest on or at the base of tombstones; occasionally, a shell border outlines the grave plot or a row traces the ridge of the mound (Figs. 2-11, 2-12). With remarkable consistency, shells are used as grave decoration in 48 percent of the cemeteries in the Big Thicket of Southeast Texas, 44 percent of those in the Piney Woods of Northeast Texas, and 44 percent of the Cross Timbers graveyards in North Texas.[23] The practice appears too often and too widely to be explained as mere decoration. Instead, we deal here with a truly ancient custom.

All three of the major cultural groups that shaped southern culture traditionally made use of shells in funeral practices. In West Africa, for example, Nigerian Yoruba funerary party members typically threw cowries to the assembled crowd, and shells sometimes appeared as Yoruba grave decoration. Some Ghanaians made shell offerings to the dead, and along much of the old slave coast ceremonial gifts of shells at funerals were once common. A traditional Zairean belief held that the dead became white creatures living under river beds and lake bottoms. Bleached shells could symbolize both the whiteness and watery character of death. Folklorist John Vlach finds this evidence sufficiently convincing to claim that southern American shell decoration is unquestionably African in origin.[24] Significantly, the custom does appear in black graveyards in the immediate vicinity of Charleston, South Carolina—the first-ranking American port of entry for colonial blacks. At the small fishing village of McClellanville, just up the coast from Charleston, I saw bleached seashells adorning several graves in a scraped-earth black cemetery. The area around McClellanville, including nearby hamlets, seems very African to the outsider. An African origin of the custom is further suggested by the appearance of shell-covered grave mounds on St. Thomas in the Virgin Islands, where blacks form a large majority of the population.

Certain Amerindian groups also associated shells with death. Among some tribes of the

FIG. 2-8. Inverted snuff bottles, half-buried in the bare earth, outline a black's grave in Floyd Valley Cemetery, Cass County. Photo by Anita Pitchford, 1979; used with permission.

FIG. 2-9. Fresh-water mussel shells, boiled white, completely cover a grave mound in Shiloh Cemetery, near Corinth in the East Cross Timbers of Denton County. Note also the iris planted beside the grave. Photo by the author, 1974.

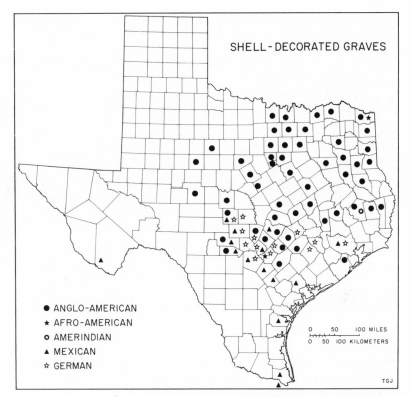

SHELL-DECORATED GRAVES

● ANGLO-AMERICAN
★ AFRO-AMERICAN
○ AMERINDIAN
▲ MEXICAN
☆ GERMAN

FIG. 2-10. Each symbol represents a county, but most counties have not been researched. Shell decoration seems to be confined largely to the Coastal Plain south and generally appears in conjunction with scraping and mounding. Sources: Clark, "Decoration of Graves"; Michael, "Grave Decoration"; Schroeder, "Upland Southern Burial Traditions"; Pitchford, "Cultural Influences in Cass County"; Stone, "Cemeteries in Tyler County"; and Gough, "Cemetery Tradition in Tarrant County"; communications from Vernon Schuder, John M. Vlach, Mrs. Tony H. Booth, Mrs. Jack Hogg, Carolyn Ericson, and Robert H. Almand.

FIG. 2-11. A variety of shells atop a weathered, bare-earth grave mound in Nancy Smith Cemetery, Somervell County, Texas. Photo by the author, 1979.

FIG. 2-12. Rows of bleached gastropod seashells trace the burial axis at Blue Ridge Cemetery, Collin County. The white shells atop the black prairie earth make a striking visual contrast. Photo by the author, 1980.

Southeast, mourners held river mussel shells in their hands during funeral ceremonies, and the Indian burial mounds at Cartersville, Georgia, contained engraved shells.[25] But, as in the case of West Africa, shells apparently were not normally used as above-ground grave decoration.

Sara Clark, among others, has proposed that the shell decoration custom likely originated in Europe. The practice may be derived from the pre-Christian Mediterranean and possibly dates to Cro-Magnon times thirty thousand years ago.[26] The supreme deity of the ancient Mediterranean was not a temperamental father figure like Zeus or Yahweh, but instead a great mother/love/fertility goddess. Masquerading under a variety of names—Magna Mater, Cybele, Aphrodite/Venus, Rhea, Isis, Astarte, Hera, Hathor, Demeter, and others—the mother goddess was worshipped widely through the Mediterranean lands for millennia.[27] We see her shadow there yet, in the ascendant position of the Virgin Mary in south European Christianity. Indeed, the very name "Mary" may come from *mare*, the sea, one of the names given to the goddess Venus, who was born of the sea. Venus, Isis, and Ceres were all called "Our Lady" and "Queen of Heaven," appellations today associated with the Virgin Mary.[28]

This great female deity had many symbols, among which were the shell, rose, pomegranate, dove, and snake.[29] The shell, in particular the spiraled conch, was an especially appropriate symbol, since it resembled in shape the female reproductive tract, and the cowrie had the form of the sex organ, similarities not lost on the ancients.[30] Among the duties of the mother goddess was to oversee the dead and, through her supreme powers of fertility, to assure their rebirth into the afterlife. To place a shell on or in a grave was to intercede with the great goddess in behalf of the deceased. "Let them be reborn," it begged of her, giving tangible expression to the primal desire of the bereaved. No more potent feminine symbol of eternal life can be found in any cemetery; the shell is strong "medicine," indeed. Shells are found in ancient Greek and Roman cemeteries, placed inside graves and stamped or sculpted on the exterior of tombs and sarcophagi.[31] In Roman times, the shell funerary custom spread as far as Britain and northern Spain, easily making the transition from pagan to Christian in those lands.[32] In the intervening centuries, the practice survived. Some present-day Welsh graves on the island of Anglesey are decorated with shells, and conches reportedly adorned the graves of the poor in certain English cemeteries in the 1850s.[33] English and Welsh immigrants perhaps introduced the practice to the southern Atlantic seaboard of the United States in colonial times. However, the British who colonized New England and the Middle Colonies do not seem to have been bearers of the shell custom.

Decoration Day

Scraping and decorating graves is typically accomplished for the first time each year at the annual "decoration day," "working," or "cleaning," usually held around the first of May (Fig. 2-13). Often it falls on the Saturday preceding the first Sunday in May, but the precise date varies from one cemetery to another. Representative, perhaps, is Harris Chapel Cemetery in Panola County, where "approximately 60 years ago the first day in May was set aside for graveyard working. Community people gathered to work the graves by hoeing and raking, and cleaning the cemetery."[34] County newspapers sometimes carry advance notices of the event (see box), or a sign at the cemetery may list the dates (Fig. 2-14). Two or three subsequent workings during the summer and autumn are customary.

The laborious job of scraping, as well as mounding and decoration, belong to the men, women, and children alike. The women are also responsible for preparing a noon meal, served at the cemetery. Many rural graveyards are equipped with permanent, elongated serving tables to facilitate the noon meal, and a picnic mood prevails (Fig. 2-15). Others make do with temporary tables, consisting of loose boards resting on sawhorses. The consumption of meals at the graveyard may be remotely akin to the ancient pagan practice

**RECOLLECTING A RED RIVER VALLEY
"WORKING"**

"The men go early and clear the cemetery
grounds of all weeds and grass. The women and
young folk coming later with well-filled lunch
baskets. What a feast that is spread and how
good everything is as we gather around the long
tables that have been arranged under the big
trees."

—Emma Guest Bourne, *A
Pioneer Farmer's Daughter Of
Red River Valley, Northeast
Texas*, p. 104.

FIG. 2-13. "Graveyard working" at Avinger in Cass
County, about 1906. Note the abundant bulb flowers;
the mixture of men, women, and children engaged
in the work; the two gravesheds (since destroyed);
and the adjacent board chapel. Photo in possession
of Janelle Knowles Krumbholz, obtained by Anita
Pitchford.

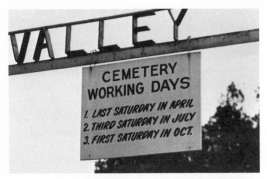

FIG. 2-14. Announcing a cult of piety, Cedar Valley Cemetery, Bell County. Photo by the author, 1980.

"LONG MOUNTAIN CEMETERY CLEANING SUNDAY"

"The cemetery will be cleaned at Long Mountain Sunday afternoon.

Persons with interest in the cemetery are urged to bring tools for cleaning and assist with the work."

—*Mason County News*, Mason, Texas, Thursday, May 10, 1979, p. 6.

FIG. 2-15. Serving tables for "decoration day" gathering, at Martin Cemetery on Trammel's Trace in Rusk County. Shaded by oak trees, these tables are permanently installed and lend an appearance of habitation to the graveyard. A tabernacle is visible on the right. Photo by the author, 1980.

found in many parts of the Old World, including Europe and Africa, of providing food for the deceased. Favorite dishes of the dead person are sometimes placed atop the grave mound in Texas, and I once observed a decorated birthday cake left in an East Cross Timbers graveyard. In a Cherokee County Anglo cemetery I saw carefully tended asparagus and blackberry plants growing on a grave, neatly surrounded by a circle of rocks.[35]

Increasingly, decoration day has become a family or community reunion, or homecoming, celebration. Many cemeteries now have "perpetual care" contracts, and hired workers do the actual maintenance, leaving the people in attendance free to visit with friends and kinfolk. In this way, a work custom born of necessity has become entirely a social event.

Traditional Flowers, Plants, and Trees

Besides the grave mound decorations, the traditional southern cemetery is adorned with a variety of flowers, plants, and trees, most of which bear an ancient, pagan symbolism. The Mediterranean mother goddess is represented by several such symbols, perhaps most notably the rosebush.[36] So common are roses in southern cemeteries that even the names of the graveyards often derive from this plant; one finds numerous "Rose Hills" and "Roselawns," and Jasper County boasts a cemetery named "Rosebloom."[37] I have found rosebushes growing in the majority of southern folk cemeteries in Texas, both along surrounding fences and on individual graves. For example, rose bushes appear in all twenty-seven traditional cemeteries inspected in Cass County.[38]

The link of the rose to the mother goddess is well known, for this flower appears in many surviving depictions of her. Demeter or Isis are often shown riding on a rose-wheeled cart, while in Rome the Magna Mater's attendants were garlanded with roses.[39] We still associate roses with motherhood, particularly on Mother's Day, when offspring wear them to church. The Virgin Mary inherited the rose

symbol from her prototype and is herself the Rose of Sharon. Often in paintings the Madonna is shown in conjunction with roses.[40] Not surprisingly, then, the rosebush became a typical European cemetery plant, particularly in the provinces once ruled by Rome, including England.[41]

The lily, derived according to Mediterranean mythology from the milk of Hera and later well established as a symbol of the Madonna, is also a common southern cemetery plant. It seemingly made a transition from paganism similar to that of the rose.[42] Lilies grow in over 40 percent of the Cass County graveyards, probably a representative proportion for all traditional southern cemeteries in Texas.[43]

In the face of such diverse symbolic evidence, it is difficult to deny that the Magna Mater occupies a prominent, if forgotten, place in the southern folk cemetery. Her cult was the last to give way to Christianity in Rome, and her worship was particularly strong among the common folk.[44] The early church fathers renounced Magna Mater, forcing her to hide, to fashion disguises, to adopt aliases. They thought they were done with her, but popular, millennia-old deities do not die so easily. All these centuries she remained among us, and our cemeteries provided one of her secret refuges.

By no means do the rose and lily complete the list of typical southern cemetery plants. Evergreens, irises, crape myrtles, gardenias, azaleas, and nandinas all abound, and occasionally one sees holly, yews, and magnolias (Figs. 2-1, 2-9). Of these, the evergreen, represented in Texas by the cedar or juniper, appears most consistently. For example, evergreens are planted in seventeen of eighteen rural cemeteries inspected in Montague County, in twenty-one of twenty-eight in Tyler County, in twenty-four of twenty-seven in Cass County, and in all twenty-two investigated in Grayson County.[45] The same is true across most of the South and, in fact, throughout most of the eastern United States and western Europe.[46] "Evergreen" is the fourth most popular cemetery name in the United States and ranks first for graveyards established before 1914.[47] The origin of this symbolism may also lie in the ancient Mediterranean, where the cedar was known as the abode of death, a tradition derived from the Osiris legend. Osiris' coffin was hidden in a cedar of Lebanon, where mother goddess Isis discovered it.[48] Another possible source of the custom is the pagan Germanic veneration of the needleleaf evergreen as a symbol of eternal life, the same veneration that gave us the Christmas tree.[49] In either case, the evergreen custom is clearly pre-Christian, and its presence in the cemeteries of Texas represents another remarkable survival of an ancient custom. The yew, an evergreen found commonly in British cemeteries, possibly because of its longevity or purple (death-colored) leaves, appears only rarely in the southern cemetery.[50] I have seen only one in a rural Texas graveyard—at Scottsville in Harrison County. The same is true of holly. Indeed, the failure to transfer some major cemetery plants from Europe to the South raises as many questions as do the successful diffusions. Why, for example, is the cypress lacking, the major cemetery tree of Greece and one sacred to the mother goddess, and why do we not have the traditional British willows?[51]

The custom of placing flowers and flowering shrubs or trees in cemeteries seemingly comes from the ancient Mediterranean and Middle East. Flowers were found, for example, in King Tut's tomb.[52] Deeply ingrained in southern cemetery custom, the use of flowers has spread to new varieties over the years. The traditional rose and lily have been joined by the gardenia, magnolia, azalea, bluebonnet, crape myrtle, nandina, and a host of others. Certainly, it would be wrong to imply any connection between the deciduous crape myrtle, a fairly recent East Indian introduction, and the evergreen Mediterranean myrtle, a plant sacred to Demeter and widely used in ancient Greek funeral ceremony and grave decoration.[53] The two plants, despite the similarity of name, do not even belong to the same genus.

The iris, especially common in southern cemeteries, is perhaps best interpreted as simply another representative of the traditional

AN EDITORIAL CONCERNING THE METHODIST CHURCHYARD

"... Our grave yard is greatly neglected—*barbarously so.* It has no more of the attention proper for such a place, than savages would give it, for no flowers are planted, no mound is raised, no stones are placed upon the graves, to denote that those who lie there, are cared for, or remembered. Neither the yard, nor the single graves, with two exceptions, are enclosed—the grass grows rank ... *where the cattle do not tramp it down,* but even upon the graves themselves, the cattle tramp, if it suits them.

"All this should be reformed. The church yard should be substantially enclosed ... The Weeping Willow, the China and some Evergreens should be planted out—and ... roses to make cheerful ... those little hillocks which are the last homes of all the human race."
—*Northern Standard,*
Clarksville, Texas, November 28, 1846, p. 2.

WALDROP CEMETERY

"Legend says that the Gentry family passed by a hill of cedars near the road leading to their home on the Old Pinehill Road, in 1872. The mother, Jemima, remarked that she wanted to be buried in that grove of cedars. A few weeks later, June 18, 1872, Mrs. Gentry died, and the owners of the land, the Waldrops, gave permission for her to be buried in the cedar grove."
—*A History of Panola County, Texas, 1819–1978,*
p. 100.

flower custom. It possesses the added advantages of helping hold the scraped earth in place and requiring little care. However, some Texas rural folk ascribe a Christian symbolism to the iris. Growing in clusters, they say, its pointed blades collectively resemble palm fronds, symbolizing Palm Sunday and Christ's last journey into Jerusalem. Too, some identify the iris with the Nile reeds that hid the infant Moses. The flower of the iris was an ancient Egyptian regal symbol but seemingly had no funerary significance there.

Orientation and Spatial Arrangement

In its internal spatial arrangement, the traditional southern cemetery is a mixture of order and chaos. Graves are often strewn about in a rather disorderly manner, in staggered rows, separate clusters, and freestanding sites. In places, the choice of location for burial seems to have been almost purely random. Chaos is most apparent in black graveyards, but southern whites share in great measure this affinity for spatial disorder.

Superimposed upon the randomness is an unfailing orientation, as certain a compass as the pole star. Nearly all southern folk cemeteries have the graves aligned on an east-west axis, and burials are made with feet to the east.[54] A Christian symbolism is attached to this practice by most rural folk. The east, they say, is the direction of Jerusalem, of the second coming, and archangel Gabriel's horn will sound from that quarter.[55] In order to be facing Christ when they rise from their graves on Judgment Day, the dead must lie with their feet to the east.[56] In many Texas cemeteries, one or two graves are aligned on a north-south axis, a posthumous punishment meted out to those who sinned extraordinarily, incurring a debt to society that will be paid on Judgment Day when the hapless soul rises facing the wrong direction.

The origin of the traditional southern burial orientation is found in Europe. One finds in Great Britain both the preferred feet-to-east position and the punitive north-south alignment for wrongdoers, notably suicides.[57] Indeed, the custom may be largely restricted to

the British Isles. In Wales, for example, the east wind is still today called "the wind of the dead men's feet."[58] Preference for the east may well have a pagan antecedent in the sun worship cults once widespread in Europe. The cult of sun god Sol Invictus was widespread in the Roman Empire at the advent of Christianity and lent to the new faith both this god's holy day, *Sun*day, as the Christian sabbath and his birthday, the winter solstice, as Christ's nativity date. He could also have provided the traditional Christian burial position. Perhaps an echo of this origin is heard in the claim by a minority of rural Texans that the feet-to-east burial allows the dead to face the rising sun. A similar explanation is occasionally encountered elsewhere in the South.[59]

Africa also offers a possible antecedent for the traditional southern burial alignment. No consistent orientation was employed among pagans in most of West Africa, though some tribes buried males facing east and females west, but among the Nagwas of Ghana both sexes were interred facing east, and the same was true in the Congo Basin of Central Africa. The north-south interment of suicides has also been observed in the Congo area. In Africa and Afro-America, east-west is regarded as the direction of the earth and therefore positive, while north-south is an evil axis. Roots growing north or south are used for malevolent purposes.[60]

Traditional Amerindian burial alignment apparently was not influential in shaping the custom of the South. An east-west axis was not uncommon in pre-Columbian America, but the head normally faced west, the direction of the spirit trail.[61]

Husband and wife also have traditional positions in the southern folk cemetery. The man is supposed to be buried to the right, or south, of the woman (Fig. 2-16). Almost every Texas folk cemetery offers exceptions to the rule, but generally over two-thirds of the married couples are interred in this arrangement. Among Anglos and blacks, I have never encountered a percentage lower than sixty, and in some cemeteries 100 percent of the married couple interments adhere to the tradition. Other Texas ethnic groups, including

Germans, Czechs, Poles, and Mexicans, do not employ this custom. Husband-to-the-right burial apparently derives from a British Christian folk-belief that Eve was created from the left side of Adam.[62] Left and left-handedness were traditionally, even in pre-Christian times, stigmatized in European culture and our word "sinister" comes from the Latin for left-handed. Because Eve ate the forbidden apple, woman apparently became associated in the folk mind with the sinister side. Woman's left-sided burial in the South duplicates her position at the taking of wedding vows and her traditional place in the nuptial bed.

A universal trait of the southern folk cemetery in Texas is the subdivision into family plots.[63] Family ties are clearly a very important factor in the spatial arrangement of burials. In fact, the majority of traditional southern cemeteries began as private family graveyards and a great many remain such to the present. But even the multifamily cemeteries are clearly segregated by surname and blood kinship. Often fences, curbing, or rows of bricks mark the confines of the family plots (Fig. 2-17). Europe offers no satisfactory model for this practice. The strength of Anglo family and clan ties in the South, fostered by frontier isolation, likely provides the explanation. Another possible source of the practice is Africa. For example, among the Ashanti peoples of Ghana, each village had several segregated clan cemeteries called *samanpow*, or "thicket of ghosts." Sometimes these clan cemeteries were separated from one another by pole or stick fences. Such graveyards were typically established within the compound of the earliest known ancestor, a custom strikingly similar to that of the American South.[64] In coastal South Carolina and Georgia, the black desire for burial in the family plot is almost compulsive, based in the fear that interment elsewhere causes the spirit of the deceased to wander.[65]

Many southern cemeteries are also compartmentalized on the basis of race. Blacks and whites often share the same burial ground, but generally the two will occupy different quarters of the graveyard. For example, at

---

AT BRAZOS POINT CEMETERY, JOHNSON COUNTY

"Do you know why they bury people facing east and west? Well, it's because when Jesus comes, He is going to come from the east and that way, when people rise up to meet Him, they will be facing Him.

"Know why they bury some facing north and south? Because they probably did something bad. And up yonder is buried that man. He was sparking this woman, and this man told him not to come back. He did. And, that man shot him dead right off of his horse."

—Jon McConal, "Cemetery Working: A Link with the Past," *Fort Worth Star Telegram*, Saturday, July 16, 1977, p. 1b, quoting a Brazos Point informant.

FIG. 2-16. This view of the west side of a tombstone in Chinns Chapel Cemetery, Denton County, shows the traditional burial position of husband and wife. The husband lies to the right (south). Photo by the author, 1974.

FIG. 2-17. Family plots, a basic internal spatial arrangement of the traditional southern burial ground, are clearly marked by masonry curbing at Nancy Smith Cemetery, Somervell County. Photo by the author, 1979.

Mount Zion in Panola County, where many of my maternal ancestors lie buried, the black section is segregated by a fence. In some other burial grounds, the separation is less rigid. A talkative rural Brazos County white man, whose work at Reliance Cemetery I interrupted one spring day, passed on to me the local story that "it was nigras that was buried here first," but he could not say exactly where the graves of the blacks lay and appeared unconcerned about maintaining a separate-but-equal racial status for the dead. Many Anglo-Texan cemeteries also contain a few Mexican graves, a common occurrence in central and western parts of the state, and the Hispanic burials normally cluster in one corner of the yard. In at least one instance that I am aware of, southern Anglos segregate themselves by religious denomination, with Baptist burials grouped on the southern end of the graveyard, separated by a wide *cordon sanitaire* from Cumberland Presbyterians in the northeastern corner.[66]

Lack of Sanctity

Southern cemeteries, in keeping with British dissenter Protestant tradition, do not occupy sanctified ground. John Wesley, for example, opposed the consecration of burial grounds as "a mere relic of Romish superstition."[67] No preferential distinction is made between graveyards situated adjacent to chapels and those that are not. Even those graveyards associated with rural churches usually predate the establishment of the congregation, and a great many church-related burial grounds evolved from private family cemeteries. Typically, the names of the rural cemeteries reflect the lack of sanctity, as is seen in such Texas graveyards as "Dark Corner" (Jack County), "Sandy" (Blanco County), and "Lonesome Dove" (Tarrant County). My favorite Texas exception to this secular naming pattern is "Little Hope Cemetery" in Wood County, where John Calvin's predestinarianism seemingly prevailed (Fig. 2-18).

Surviving as a relict of burial sanctity is the practice, almost universal, of siting southern cemeteries on high ground or slopes.[68] "In every case of observed cemeteries," wrote Anita Pitchford concerning Cass County, "the location is on the highest hill or most elevated slope in the immediate area," and one graveyard occupies the highest point in the county, in the chain of hills called the Cusseta Mountains.[69] The veneration of high places is far older than Christianity and permeates diverse religions around the world.

Burial in unsanctified ground is a clear departure from western European custom. In such countries as England and Germany, the yard adjacent to the church was traditionally regarded as the most appropriate place for burial. The Catholic Irish often bury people inside the ruins of abandoned churches. In the American South, many frontiersmen had little concern for religion, and few churches existed in the early years of settlement, opening the way for unsanctified burial. But even the devout could not transport their dead from isolated homesteads over poor roads and trails to distant churchyards in the heat of southern summers. The unsanctified private family cemetery was a practical frontier necessity.

A vestige of European desire for sanctity and the presence of a church near the burial ground is seen in the frequently encountered tabernacles situated within chapelless south-

FIG. 2-18. John Calvin was right, after all, according to this predestinarian graveyard name in Wood County. Photo by the author, 1980.

ern cemeteries (Fig. 2-19). These roofed, open-sided structures have benches or pews and are the scene of funeral ceremonies and social gatherings at the annual spring "decoration day." They inject an element of Christianity and sanctity into a largely secular or pagan setting.

Gravehouses

Similar to the tabernacle in appearance, but smaller and quite different in function and origin, is the gravehouse or graveshed (Fig. 2-20).[70] These diminutive roofed structures, their sides either open or partially enclosed by pickets or lattices, cover normal in-ground burials and should not be confused with false crypts or the above-ground cemeteries of the Louisiana French (Fig. 1-2). Some older examples are built of notched logs. Rarely are more than several graves covered by such sheds in any particular cemetery, and many graveyards have none. In Cass County, for example, gravehouses occur in only four of the twenty-seven cemeteries surveyed, generally singly, comparable to the appearance in three of twenty-eight Tyler County graveyards (Figs. 2-13, 2-21).[71] Often they stand over the graves of the more prominent families in the community, perhaps serving as a status symbol (Fig. 2-22).

In the South, gravehouses are found among whites, blacks, and Indians alike, especially the latter. The gravehouse custom is particularly common in the Upland South, in a belt stretching westward from Tennessee to Oklahoma (Fig. 2-23). Its major concentration east of Texas lies in the highlands north of the Gulf Coastal Plain, north of the area where such features as scraping and shell decoration are common. We must assume, therefore, that its origins were also different.

Gravehouses bear some resemblance to rubble-filled, stone-slab "hogback" graves in Britain, and wooden huts cover the resting place of wealthy persons in parts of Sweden, but these are unlikely prototypes.[72] More promising are some pagan practices in West Africa. A European traveler describing the customs in Ghana about 1700 noted that "the *Negroes*

generally build a small Cottage or Hut, or else plant a little Garden of Rice on the Grave, into which they throw several worthless Goods of the Deceased . . ."[73] Two centuries later another observer, in Nigeria, described how most pagan tribes "erect thatched shelters over the graves of chiefs," a custom still practiced in Angola in the 1930s.[74] Elsewhere in West Africa, many tribes buried the dead in the earthen floor of their dwellings.[75] When viewing a bare earth grave covered with a shed in an East Texas cemetery, one can only be struck by the similarity to the African custom. However, gravehouses are much less common among blacks than among whites and Indians.

The gravehouse is more likely of Amerindian origin. It is found among many eastern tribes, such as the Creeks (including the Coushattas), Shawnees, Choctaws, Cherokees, and Seminoles (Fig. 2-24). Many other Indian tribes outside the South built similar sheds, including some as far afield as the Midwest, New England, and the Pacific Northwest.[76] John R. Swanton, the prime authority on southeastern Indians, described several possible antecedent forms of the gravehouse. Some groups, for example, buried their priests in houses, then burned the structure. Others collected bones of the dead in charnel houses, prior to collective burial in mounds.[77] Some Choctaw elders told Swanton that their tribe formerly placed the deceased on the ground in the yard of the dwelling and erected a little house over it during the decomposition of the body. Choctaws also buried some dead inside their former dwelling, paralleling an African custom.[78] The gravehouses of displaced southeastern tribes in Oklahoma have been described as "a custom of long ago to protect and comfort the spirit of the deceased."[79] The southeastern Indians practice the gravehouse custom to a greater extent than do either whites or blacks. In some of their cemeteries, sheds cover nearly all the older graves.[80] Curiously, though, the Alabama-Coushatta reservation graveyard in Polk County, Texas, lacks such sheds. Still, the weight of evidence and present usage strongly suggest an Amerindian origin, with diffusion accomplished through

FIG. 2-19. A fine tabernacle in a McLennan County graveyard in Central Texas. Tabernacles are often present if a chapel or church is not located adjacent to the burial ground, lending some small measure of unintended sanctity to the site. Probably tabernacles are an echo of the ancestral western European custom of churchyard burial. The tabernacle is used for funerals and for memorial services held at the cemetery working. Photo by the author, 1980.

FIG. 2-20. Two small, decaying gravehouses in the Mills Cemetery, Garland, Texas, covering graves of the Mills family. The picket walls are typical. Photo by the author, 1977.

FIG. 2-21. A beautifully maintained East Texas gravehouse in Cornett Cemetery, Cass County. Notice also the false crypt and enclosing fence. Photo by Anita Pitchford, 1979; used with permission.

FIG. 2-22. An ornate "Victorian" gravehouse protects an Anglo-American burial at the old city cemetery in La Grange, Fayette County. Clearly, such structures could be status symbols. Photo by the author, 1980.

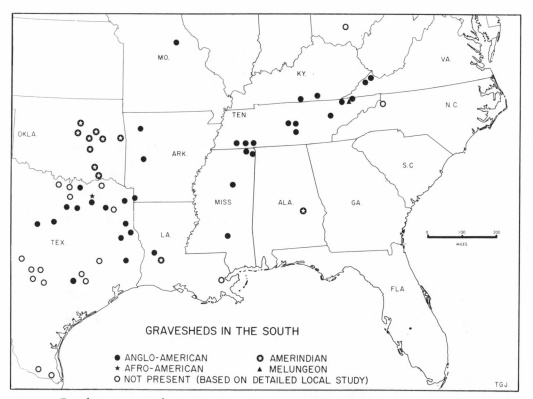

GRAVESHEDS IN THE SOUTH

● ANGLO-AMERICAN   ✪ AMERINDIAN
★ AFRO-AMERICAN   ▲ MELUNGEON
○ NOT PRESENT (BASED ON DETAILED LOCAL STUDY)

TGJ

FIG. 2-23. Gravehouses seem to be most common in the Upper South and seemingly are derived from eastern Indian tribes. Each symbol represents a county, but most counties have not been researched. Cited sources: Ball, "Middle Tennessee Gravehouses"; Cozzens, "A Cherokee Graveyard"; Corn, "Covered Graves"; Cobb, "Gravehouses in Tennessee"; Price, "Providing Shelters for Graves"; J. Winston Coleman, Jr. (ed.), *Kentucky: A Pictorial History*, p. 188; George F. Fielder, Jr., et al., *Historic Sites Reconnaissance of the Oak Ridge Reservation*, pp. 31–36; [Federal Writer's Project], *Mississippi*, pp. 450–451; Albrecht, "Religious Material Culture"; Gough, "Cemetery Tradition in Tarrant County"; Stone, "Cemeteries in Tyler County"; Templeton, "Folk Cemeteries"; Pitchford, "Cultural Influences in Cass County"; communications from Tom Harvey, Mrs. Jack Hogg, Vernon Schuder, Mrs. Tony H. Booth, Carolyn Ericson, and John B. Rehder.

FIG. 2-24. Choctaw gravehouses at Homer Chapel in Choctaw County, Oklahoma. Such structures are most common among Indians in the South. Some of these are of very recent construction. Photo by the author, 1979.

intermarriage with whites and blacks. It is perhaps significant that the Melungeons, a mixed-blood group of partial Indian ancestry living in the mountains of Tennessee, build gravehouses (see Fig. 2-23).

Fences and Lichgates

The large majority of southern folk cemeteries are enclosed by a fence, in contrast to Midwestern, New England, or even Kentucky graveyards, which are usually unfenced. In Cass County, East Texas, twenty-three of twenty-seven cemeteries have a surrounding fence, comparable to fourteen enclosed Anglo graveyards of a total of eighteen in Denton and Cooke counties, North Texas.[81] The lack of such an enclosure, or its poor repair, can be an embarrassment to the local community or family, and fund-raising drives are often held to build or improve fences. Even individual graves or family plots within the typical southern cemetery in Texas are sometimes fenced (Fig. 2-25). This compulsion to enclose the burial ground apparently derives from British tradition, for enclosing walls are ancient in Britain, possibly dating to early Celtic Christianity. The church lent its support to the custom in 1229, when an English bishop required all cemeteries to be walled and forbade the grazing of livestock in the churchyard.[82] I have observed the same revulsion toward animals in the cemetery among rural Anglo-Texans.

FIG. 2-25. An elaborate metal fence, clearly in the nonfolk tradition, surrounds a family plot in John Robin Heard Cemetery, Cass County. The desire to enclose graveyards and even individual plots is very strong in the Lower South. Photo by Anita Pitchford, 1979; used with permission.

Also common both in Britain and Texas is the Anglo-Saxon *lichgate*, or "corpse gate," a ceremonial entranceway to the cemetery spanned by an overhead arch (Figs. 2-18, 2-26).[83] The funeral procession passes beneath the lichgate, while everyday visitors to the graveyard enter by way of smaller, unarched gates. In Britain the lichgates are often rather elaborate, containing a gabled roof (Fig. 2-27), but in Texas and the South they usually consist of a steel or wooden span, to which is normally affixed a sign showing the name of the cemetery. The original reason for employing lichgates is unclear, but they may be symbolic of departure from the world of the living. Among the Georgia coastal blacks, the funeral procession stops outside the gate while the leader asks the dead for permission to enter.[84]

A Cultural Index

The traditional southern cemetery, then, contains a disorderly array of European, African, and Amerindan material culture. In the main, the customs and artifacts displayed are pagan and, almost without exception, the original symbolic meaning is unknown to the rural people who maintain these graveyards. They have no knowledge of the ancient fertility cults and animism that provided the individual elements of their funerary culture. They do not know they are perpetuating millennia-old practices.

If we use the traditional cemetery as an index to the relative importance of contributions by Europeans, Africans, and Amerindians to southern culture, then the preeminent position of the European becomes apparent (Table 2-1). To be sure, it is a creolized European influence, one drawing both upon the Mediterranean hearth of European civilization and upon the Germanic-Celtic northwest. Our morbid index also suggests a significant African contribution, one greater than the enslaved condition of those immigrants would lead us to expect and more important than students of southern culture have heretofore been willing to ascribe to blacks.

I know of no overall assessment of Amerindian influence on the folkways of the South. The rural graveyard provides evidence of a modest native American imprint. While somewhat less significant than African influence, the Indian contribution certainly exists. Indian blood is claimed by a sizable number of "white" southerners, and we should expect the genetic input to be accompanied by a roughly equal measure of cultural ingredients.

The message of the folk cemetery, for those who would read it, is that there is a lot of European, a fair amount of African, and more than a trace of Indian in all southerners, regardless of their skin color. In the cultural sense the people of the South have much in

FIG. 2-26. A fine wrought-iron *lichgate*, at the entrance to a Cass County cemetery. The lichgate and enclosing fence are British in origin. Photo by Anita Pitchford, 1979; used with permission.

common with each other. For three centuries the three groups exchanged ideas and genes, creolizing the culture to a remarkable degree. Nowhere is that blending more apparent than in the places we have set aside for our dead. These traditional graveyards are not merely repositories for our dead, but museums full of reminders from our ancient past and distant, diverse ancestral homelands.

Another aspect of the traditional southern cemetery, not considered in this chapter, is the use of tombstones. These markers, and the inscriptions on them, provide the subject matter for Chapter 3.

"ARCHWAY AND GATE ERECTED AT CEMETERY"

"During January 1979, an archway and gate were placed at the Millett Cemetery by Peggy Poston in memory of her husband Tilmon T. Poston who died on September 20, 1976. The chain link fence bordering the highway was contributed by a sister, Venus Poston Turk, and a brother and sister-in-law, Sun and Thursie Poston."

—*Cotulla Record*, Cotulla, La Salle County, Thursday, July 5, 1979, p. 1.

FIG. 2-27. A British lichgate at Horley, Surrey, England, the probable prototype of the southern and Texan arched cemetery gateway. Photo by the author, 1978.

Traditional Southern Grave Markers

TRADITIONAL GRAVE MARKERS in the American South range from humble home-made wooden boards or crudely shaped slabs of native stone, upon which are perhaps scrawled a few cryptic symbols and a terse epitaph, to beautifully crafted stones adorned with well-formed letters and designs. These, in time, were largely succeeded by a variety of commercially made tombstones, though some folk markers are still being made today.

The pagan symbolism of the southern folk cemetery, catalogued in Chapter 2, extends also to these modest grave markers, folk and commercial alike. Indeed, the mere use of an upstanding grave marker commemorates an ancient pagan European custom, both British and Mediterranean, the original symbolism of which was likely phallic. The popular round-topped "tablet" shape of grave marker, found in both wood and stone in Texas and the South, even retains a vaguely phallic config-uration (Fig. 3-1). As such, the masculine grave marker provides a counterpart for the possibly gynosymbolic shell, lending the bur-ial place a potentially sexual meaning—one seemingly forgotten countless generations ago by distant ancestors of the present-day Protes-tant practitioners. But regardless of the level of craftsmanship or the long-obsolete symbol-ism, the southern folk grave marker remains simple, unpretentious, and largely unadorned. John Calvin dictated long ago that it be so.[1]

The tombstone, anchoring the western end of the grave mound, is counterbalanced by a smaller footstone erected at the opposite, eastern end. Collectively, the abundant array of head and foot markers presents a spatial pattern at once chaotic and ordered. The indi-vidual graves are often strewn about in a rather disorderly manner, but the unfailing di-rectional devotion to the east-west solar axis introduces an aspect of alignment and order, one most impressive in the early morning and late evening, when the markers cast accordant reflections and parallel shadows through the graveyard.

Wooden Grave Markers

Some of the oldest folk grave markers in Texas and the American South are wooden.[2] These include a gamut from simple stakes or two-by-fours to milled, sawn boards of pine or cedar measuring one-by-six to one-by-ten (Fig. 3-2). The latter are rarely left with a straight top edge but are instead usually shaped to be rounded tablets, Gothic inverted Vs, figures resembling a human above-waist profile, and other forms (Figs. 3-3, 3-4).

Relatively few wooden grave markers sur-vive in rural and small-town Texas. Rot, in-sects, and fire had their way with the large majority, while others succumbed to afflu-ence, replaced by commercial stones as a reflection of growing family wealth. The great-est surviving concentrations of wooden mark-ers seem to be in central and northern Texas, in both the Blacklands and the Cross Tim-bers. They are even seen in rural cemeteries around towns like McKinney and Sulphur Springs, among prosperous prairie farmers. Perhaps termites and carpenter ants are less

FIG. 3-1. These homemade stone tablets in a Central Texas folk cemetery, though crudely shaped, strongly suggest the original phallic symbolism of upright tombstones. Cedar Valley Cemetery, Bell County, photo by the author, 1980.

FIG. 3-2. A crude wooden stake grave marker, approximately 2″ × 6″, stands in Bethlehem Cemetery, Collin County. Photo by the author, 1980.

FIG. 3-3. A nicely cut wooden tablet marker in the Old City Cemetery, Denton, Texas. Photo by the author, 1974.

FIG. 3-4. A wooden marker cut in what may be the stylistic shape of a person, in a "scraped" portion of the old city cemetery, La Grange, Fayette County. The inscription has become illegible. Compare the shape of this marker to the "male" stone in Fig. 3-10. This shape possibly reflects African influence. Photo by the author, 1980.

active there than in the red clays and yellow sands of the humid forested districts of East Texas.

Texas' wooden headboards, in common with other traits of the traditional southern burial ground, cross racial lines and appear in the graveyards of whites, blacks, and Amerindians alike (Fig. 3-5).[3] The diffusionary trail of wooden markers leads to Texas from across the South. Examples appear among the highland whites of Middle Tennessee, the "crackers" of Alabama's coastal plain, and the blacks residing along South Carolina's shore.[4] The Texan examples, in most design respects, duplicate the wooden markers of the eastern regions of the South. From the Atlantic seaboard, the path leads back to England, where wooden grave markers were very common in some shires as late as the seventeenth century, when emigrants were departing in droves for the southern colonies.[5] Earlier prototypes, from Roman times, occur in the Mediterranean peninsulas.

Stone Markers

Another early, traditional southern grave marker is the fieldstone.[6] Completely unworked and often bearing no inscription, these rude stones offer greater permanence and durability than do wooden markers. Wherever stone outcrops at the surface or is available beneath a shallow soil, particularly in the hilly and mountainous portions of the South, fieldstones appear frequently as grave markers. Many were obtained in the process of digging the very graves they commemorate. Ferrous sandstone is the most common type encountered in Texas cemeteries, but limestone examples can also be found (Fig. 3-6). While these fieldstones are left in their natural condition, the mourners often select particular shapes. Sharply pointed stones are commonly chosen, presumably because of their Gothic profiles. One of the best assemblages of uninscribed fieldstone grave markers in Texas is found in the dense cedar shade of LaSalle Church of Christ Cemetery in eastern Limestone County. Still completely scraped, LaSalle cemetery, with row upon row

FIG. 3-5. Wooden headboard and footboard in the
Alabama-Coushatta Indian graveyard, Polk County.
Note also the use of shell decoration, scraping, and
mounding. Photo courtesy of Professor Francis E.
Abernethy of Stephen F. Austin State University,
Nacogdoches, Texas.

of unworked ferrous sandstone markers, in
1980 had the look of the frontier about it.

If the bereaved family is literate, the fieldstone will bear a terse inscription, crudely but
lovingly scratched in the soft native rock.
Often this amounts to nothing more than the
initials of the deceased, but some consist of a
few phonetically spelled words containing
poorly or incorrectly formed letters, together
with a date (Fig. 3-7).[7]

One step above the fieldstone in the southern folk tradition are slabs of native rock
hewn by hand into any one of several artificial shapes, particularly square-topped blocks,
rounded tablets, and Gothic points (Figs. 3-1,
3-8, 3-9). Two of the most remarkable carved

FIG. 3-6. Unshaped fieldstone markers, lacking inscriptions, in the southern Anglo graveyard at Cedar Valley in Bell County. Such markers were once dominant. Photo by the author, 1980.

sandstone grave markers in Texas stand neglected, side by side, in the overgrown Old Bethel burial ground in Panola County. Fashioned in antebellum times by slaves to stand over the graves of a white minister and his wife, the stones take the stylistic shape of male and female figures (Fig. 3-10). No inscriptions appear on the two markers, even though such carefully shaped stones normally do bear at least the name of the deceased. The human effigy shape may be of African origin, since it appears, generally in wood, among blacks in Texas, Georgia, and perhaps elsewhere in the South.[8]

Here and there, in individual southern graveyards, one encounters true craftsman-

FIG. 3-7. Inscribed fieldstone grave marker in the Indian Creek Cemetery, Cooke County. Commemorating a white infant who died in 1898, the sandstone marker is decorated with an abstract design around the border, possibly intended to be a stylistic wreath. Photo by the author, 1980.

FIG. 3-8. A native ferrous sandstone slab carefully shaped into a Gothic pointed grave marker in the Swisher Cemetery, Denton County. Note the scribed guidelines and the incorrectly formed letters. Such markers, in a variety of shapes, are very typical of southern folk graves in Texas. Photo by the author, 1980.

FIG. 3-9. A nicely crafted folk tombstone in the Cooper Creek Cemetery, Denton County. A double tablet in bas relief adds to the impressiveness of this native sandstone marker. The metathesis typical of Hill Southern speech caused the craftsman to fall short in his effort to spell "memory." Photo by the author, 1980.

ship in the shaping and carving of native stone markers. These tombstones are beautifully and symmetrically formed, containing carefully lettered, correctly spelled inscriptions (Fig. 3-11). Such delights are all too rare, for the southern rural folk, unlike their counterparts in New England, apparently did not place a great value on tombstone artistry (or on education).[9] The professional or semi-professional stone carver was uncommon in the South; emotion, poverty, and tradition directed that the markers should, instead, be made and erected by the bereaved.

The use of unworked or shaped stones as commemorative markers for the deceased bears a venerable European magico-symbolic meaning. The ancients, awed by the seeming permanence of rocks and stones, understandably associated them with immortality. British megalithic burials 4,500 years old are covered with flat stones and marked by upright stones inserted, some at the phallic angle, in the ground. The early Irish, among others, believed that these rocks and stones absorbed the souls of the dead, providing them an eternal home.

FIG. 3-10. Sandstone markers, reputedly fashioned in the 1840s by a slave artisan, commemorate an East Texas white married couple. The "broad-shouldered" stone on the left (south) of the picture is for the husband, Isaac Reed, alongside the curvaceous marker for his wife. The stones stand in Panola County, in the neglected, overgrown Old Bethel graveyard, which contains a mixture of white and black burials. Photo by the author, 1980.

Brick, Cement, and Metal Folk Markers

Wooden and native stone markers dominated the southern folk tradition before about 1900, but since that time diversification has occurred. Many folk markers erected in the twentieth century consist of unadorned bricks or slabs of molded cement.[10] The bricks, both homemade and commercially manufactured, are set upright in the sand at the head and foot of the grave mound (Fig. 3-12). Even when more elaborate headstones are present, bricks often remain as footstones. Common sources of these bricks were the chimneys that were dismantled when cast-iron stoves replaced open fireplaces in many southern homes after about 1880.

When commercial cement became widely and inexpensively available early in the 1900s, many rural folk began using it to fashion grave markers. Poured into a mold of the desired shape, the cement is allowed to begin hardening before an inscription is written with a stylus, stick, or some other pointed instrument (Fig. 3-13). Any suburban child who has inscribed graffiti in new sidewalks after the workmen departed the scene knows this process. Marbles, glass fragments, or trinkets are sometimes pressed into the damp cement marker as decoration, particularly if the deceased is a child.

Another, much less common, material used in making twentieth-century southern folk grave markers is metal. Sheet iron and solder are worked to produce the desired shape and lettering (Fig. 3-14). When weathering turns the metal rusty, these markers take on the reddish-brown color of the ferrous sandstone used so widely in the earlier folk period.

The advent of commercial, precut markers of exotic stone signaled the gradual decline of folk types. In the more prosperous county seats, some commercial stones appeared even before the Civil War, and the spread into rural graveyards began in earnest after about 1880. In some remote rural cemeteries, folk-made markers continued to prevail well into the twentieth century, particularly among blacks, but the commercial types now dominate

FIG. 3-11. A beautifully crafted homemade marker of native sandstone, Chinns Chapel Cemetery, Denton County. Such perfection of symmetry and flawlessly formed letters are rare on southern folk tombstones in Texas. Photo by the author, 1974.

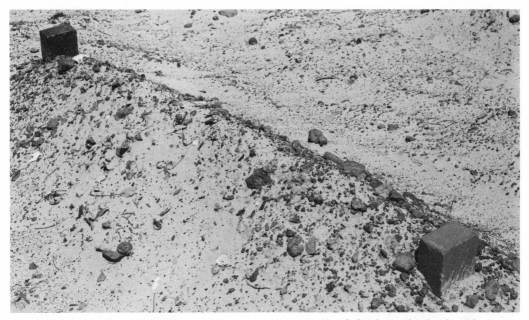

FIG. 3-12. Simple bricks used as head and foot markers, Indian Creek Cemetery, Cooke County. This custom is very widespread in the southern folk cemeteries of Texas. Photo by the author, 1980.

FIG. 3-13. A homemade cement folk grave marker in the Cedar Valley Cemetery, Bell County. Black paint, applied recently, heightens the visibility of the inscriptions scratched in the cement and adds to the somber appearance of the marker. Note the scraped, mounded grave. Photo by the author, 1980.

FIG. 3-14. Sheet-metal tablet-type folk marker, with solder lettering, Trinity Cemetery, Denton County. The marker, now rusted, bears no date. Note the curled edge. Photo by the author, 1980.

most burial grounds. Homemade cement markers represent the last significant survival of the southern folk tombstone tradition in Texas today.

In shape and size, many commercial tombstones are similar to the folk types that preceded them, but a variety of new styles are also present. Over twenty generic types of commercial stones, each with numerous subtypes, occur in Texas cemeteries. The commercial markers consist of granite, marble, and other extremely hard stones that are impervious to traditional folk cutting tools. As a consequence, the lettering must also be professionally done, completely removing gravestone preparation from the domain of the bereaved family and clan. In almost every county seat in Texas today, a professional stonecutter, his mass-produced, uninscribed "monuments" displayed in a false cemetery in the yard surrounding the place of business, awaits potential customers. Only those too poor to afford his product or sundry mavericks repulsed by the "American way of death" will not eventually patronize his shop.

Many who recognize, correctly, that traditional southern gravemarkers rarely exemplify highly developed folk art will not regret the advent of the commercial stonecutter and his exotic, machine-shaped product. Still, the homemade touch, however primitive, is infinitely more expressive of family emotions and local culture. For these reasons, we should lament the passing of the southern tradition.

Tombstone Decoration

A variety of decorations, both abstract and symbolic, appear on southern grave stones, though markers in the pure folk tradition are less likely to display such ornamentation than are early examples of commercially made stones.[11] In fact, some forms of symbolic decoration are clearly taboo in the Protestant South, in particular the Christian cross, which most of the common folk regard as "popish," an attitude derived from the Old World British Protestants.[12] Very rarely, wooden Latin crosses do appear atop southern graves,

probably a heritage of the scattering of Celtic Catholics in the Anglo population or a borrowing from neighboring Louisiana French and Hispanos. For example, Sand Ridge Cemetery, a traditional southern graveyard in Newton County, near the "Cajun" stronghold in adjacent Louisiana, displays abundant wooden crosses. Similarly, the "Seminole Negroes," a mixed black-Indian group living in and around Brackettville in Southwest Texas, commonly mark their graves with simple wooden crosses, probably a heritage of their long residence in Mexico and close association with Hispanos in the Texas borderland. Often, close inspection of wooden crosses in traditional southern graveyards reveals that they mark the burial places of a small local Hispanic minority, as at Cooper Creek Cemetery in Denton County. Only rarely does the cross in any form appear on an Anglo tombstone (Fig. 3-15).

Less understandable is the failure of southerners to use some traditionally important British Protestant tombstone symbols, such as the skull-and-crossbones, the commonest of all English graveyard symbols, the winged death's head, the six-petaled flower (or star), the hourglass, the cockleshell or scallop, and the serpent-biting-tail.[13] Even Calvinistic New Englanders, who generally shunned symbolism, developed the death's head to an art form.[14]

Instead, the most common tombstone decorations in the southern folk tradition are geometric designs and simple scribed lines. A crosshatching often covers the edges of burial stones, and borders are sometimes adorned with zig-zag or ruled lines, or perhaps an arrow or a stylistic wreath (Figs. 3-7, 3-16, 3-17). The designs sometimes resemble abstract Moslem patterns and apparently bear little or no intentional or hidden symbolism (Figs. 3-18, 3-15).

Occasionally, even on fieldstone markers, one finds hearts or hands carefully inscribed by the southern folk (Fig. 3-16). The heart, which also appears as a symbol of charity on British tombstones, is particularly common on children's graves in the South.[15] In one Tyler County rural cemetery, a rotting wooden

FIG. 3-16. A sandstone folk marker rich in decoration and symbolism, Indian Creek Cemetery, Cooke County. Note the crosshatched grid on top of the fieldstone, the hands with skyward-pointed index fingers, the heart, and the wave pattern. The stone was apparently prepared by two young brothers of the deceased, in 1898. Photo by the author, 1980.

FIG. 3-15. The undated A. J. Turnbo grave stone at Whites Chapel Methodist Cemetery, Tarrant County. Made of native sandstone, the Turnbo stone is remarkable because of the cross decoration and the cursive writing. Note also the semicircular abstract design and the scribed lines. The rhymed verse epitaph, barely legible, reads "Sweet Rest / A J Turnbo / Calm on the Bosom of thy god / fair spirit rest the[e] now / even whilst with us thy footsteps trod / his seal[?] was on thy Brow." The date 1910 was scratched later in the stone and may be correct. Photo by the author, 1980.

TABOO IN TENNESSEE

"I never seen a cross in these graveyards out here. . . . people just sorta thought it indicated Catholicism, and there's not a Catholic—never a Catholic buried in this county. . . . Our local communities out here, they just didn't put crosses. They'd just stick down a straight slab of pine."

> —A rural resident of Coffee County, Tennessee, as quoted in Donald B. Ball, "Wooden Gravemarkers: Neglected Items of Material Culture," p. 168. Reprinted with permission from *Tennessee Folklore Society Bulletin.*

FIG. 3-17. A nicely crafted homemade marker, Lonesome Dove Baptist Cemetery, Tarrant County. Note the use of hand, arrow, and open Bible decorative motifs. The structure depicted at the bottom is a steepled church, but it may represent the Heavenly home. Photo by the author, 1980.

marker cut in the shape of a heart was observed, and in the commercial phase, special
children's tombstones in the heart shape were
marketed.[16] Even so, the heart is much more
common in Texas German cemeteries than in
those of the southern people. The finger
pointed skyward, symbolizing ascent to
Heaven and sometimes inscribed "Gone
Home," is also widely employed on commercial and some folk stones (Fig. 3-16). For less
apparent reasons, a hand with downward-
pointing index finger also occurs on markers
in southern cemeteries, perhaps a depiction of
the hand of God, as if to say "you are next" or
"God wants you," in the manner of the famous World War I army recruitment poster.

Various other hand and arm symbols can be
found on southern vernacular tombstones.

The clasped hands motif presumably represents a congratulatory "welcome to Heaven"
handshake. Most of these heavenly hand
motifs have abundant English Protestant pre-
cedence.[17] My favorite Texan example of the
"hand of God" theme appears in the Cooper
Creek Cemetery near Denton. Pictured on
one child's tombstone there, dating from the
1880s, is a Heavenly cloud, from which an
arm has reached down to grab a reclining
lamb firmly by the back of the neck, prepara-
tory to lifting it upward into the Great Beyond—a classic "gotcha."

Usually in less bizarre ways, the lamb is a
favorite symbol of infantile and childhood
mortality. Many commercial stones marking
children's graves depict the figure of a reclining lamb (Fig. 3-19). I have not seen this motif
in the pure folk tradition, though the British
dissenter Protestants of the American South
revel in the Christian lamb symbolism. "Are
you washed in the blood of the Lamb?" they
ask in hymn, and, on a less gory level, the
lamb also represents innocence and youth for
them.

Another animal appearing frequently on
southern tombstones is the dove, an ancient
consort of the great Mediterranean mother
goddess and also representative, in Christian
lore, of the Holy Spirit (Fig. 3-20). The dove
was an important symbol of the Magna Mater
from very early times, and Roman-British use
of the dove on funerary monuments is well
documented.[18] In Christian art, the dove is
frequently associated with the Madonna, usually hovering above her head.[19] An eighteenth-
century revival of the dove motif in funerary
art occurred in England and eventually spread
to the American South.[20] In all probability,
the use of such a symbol on homemade folk
tombstones was inspired by the doves adorning professionally made markers that appeared in the period after about 1850, particularly in the graveyards of wealthy planters
and townfolk.

Another ancient symbol of the Magna
Mater, the rose, also finds expression in
southern tombstone decoration. From very
early commercial stones to the present, rose
blossoms, often with the thorny stem at-

FIG. 3-18. Abstract geometric designs on a small
Gothic limestone folk grave marker, Old City
Cemetery, Denton. The stone, possibly for a black
person, bears no inscription. Photo by the author,
1980.

tached, frequently appear on markers commemorating mothers (Fig. 3-21). Clearly, the
inspiration for this symbol came most directly from the southern and British folk
custom of planting roses in graveyards, as was
described in Chapter 2.[21]

Trees also appear in southern tombstone
art. The traditional British "tree of life" symbolism finds it widest Texan usage in the
ubiquitous Woodsmen of the World commercial monuments, which normally take the
shape of a sawn-off tree stump. More rarely,
Woodsmen markers take the bizarre config-
uration of a stack of stone "cordwood." The
grim reaper apparently also owns a saw and
enjoys a turn of exercise in the woodlot. Less
common in Texas, but older, are commercial
tombstones adorned with a willow tree (Fig.
3-22). These markers, perpetuating in stone
the old English custom of planting willows in
cemeteries, generally date from the 1840–
1880 period and are found mainly in county-
seat graveyards.[22] Their use in decoration may
have been encouraged by a traditional British
ballad, "The Weeping Willow," that survived
in the American South:

> "Bury me beneath the willow,
> Beneath the weeping willow tree,
> So he may know where I am sleeping,
> Perhaps some day he will weep for me."[23]

Also British in origin and well represented in
Texas folk and popular tradition is the open-
book, or Bible, symbol (Fig. 3-17).[24] In addition, Texas graveyards contain a host of
custom-made symbols, sometimes related to
the occupation of the deceased or the cause of
death. One of my Texan favorites of this type
is the 1938 stone of a 25-year-old man in
Cedar Point Cemetery, Brown County, showing a racing car with the inscription "The
Last Lap."

Simple Inscriptions

Southerners are not, and never have been,
great epitaph writers. Largely absent from
their folk tradition are the lengthy, poetic, or
even humorous inscriptions sometimes found

FIG. 3-19. The reclining-lamb design on a child's
grave, Old City Cemetery, Denton. This example
is clearly a commercially cut stone, but the lamb
motif occasionally appears on folk stones. Photo by
the author, 1980.

in New England's graveyards or the cemeteries of Anglican and Catholic portions of
the British Isles. No doubt the high rate of
illiteracy and semiliteracy is partly to blame
for the paucity of epitaphs in the South. By
way of comparison, the illiteracy rate among
adult whites in 1850 was almost 17 percent in
Texas and less than 3 percent in Vermont and
New Hampshire combined.[25] Bereaved southerners have never been under moral or social obligation to place writing on the grave
marker, and it is probably fair to say that the
majority of antebellum southern grave markers bore no inscriptions whatever.

The most primitive inscriptions found in
southern cemeteries of Texas are simply the
name, initials, or other minimal identification of the deceased. In a rural graveyard near

FIG. 3-20. The dove, one of the animal consorts of
the ancient Mediterranean mother/fertility goddess,
dominates a commercial tombstone in Scottsville,
Harrison County. Photo by the author, 1977.

FIG. 3-21. This rose blossom, a pagan symbol of the
ancient Mediterranean Magna Mater, appears on a
grave marker at Scottsville, Harrison County. Photo
by the author, 1977.

FIG. 3-22. The traditional British funerary weeping willow, depicted on an early commercial stone in the old city cemetery, La Grange, Fayette County. Photo by the author, 1980.

Denton, for example, are four unadorned square-topped stone tablets in a row. The larger stone bears only the crudely inscribed name "Hattie Settle," while the three smaller tablets on either side are each cryptically marked simply "Hattie's baby" (Fig. 3-23). A visitor is left to reconstruct in his or her imagination the tragic events that might have produced the depressing little row of stones. Did the unfortunate Hattie die giving birth to stillborn triplets? Who and where is the father? When did the tragedies occur? In this same cryptic tradition is the single word "Burnet" scratched upon a red brick "headstone" in Little Hope Cemetery, Wood County.

A bit more informative, and perhaps most typical among southern folk inscriptions, are stones bearing the initials or name of the deceased together with the dates of birth and/or death. In a county-seat graveyard in North Texas are markers reading simply:

> W B R   1897
>   ƧALIE
> 1880   WRIGHT
>   (both in Old City Cemetery,
>   Denton, Denton County)

FIG. 3-23. Rubbings of the complete, terse inscriptions on four adjacent tombstones in the Swisher Cemetery, Denton County. The visitor can only guess at the sequence of events leading to the quadruple tragedy. Rubbings by Marlis A. Jordan, 1980.

Somewhat lengthier, and also typical, is a homemade East Texas cement marker in a black cemetery commemorating:

> Miss Lucille Foster
> Born April
> 16 1909
> Past August
> 13 1945
> > (Tyler County) [26]

Many such markers reveal a desire to record the age of the deceased (and a tendency to overpunctuate):

> Emma Harris.
> Was. Bornd
> February. 16 1848.
> And. Died. Feb
> 17. 18.91. Age. 43
> Years
> > (Shiloh Cemetery, near
> > Bartonville, Denton County)

At times the need to reckon the exact age seems obsessive, and it is counted in years, months, and days:

> Cordelia Young
> died Aug. 17 1916
> 25 Years 102d
> > (Old City Cemetery,
> > Denton, Denton County)

Others reveal less concern or knowledge about exact age and date:

> B. F. Andrews
> Ab'ot 55 Ys. Old
> Died
> Dec. 17, 1905
> At Rest
> > (Trinity Cemetery, Denton
> > County)

> M A
> Hudson
> Died
> 1911
> A. 77
> > (Swisher Cemetery, Denton
> > County)

Sometimes the profession of the deceased is suggested, as in the following inscription from a black cemetery:

> Prof. C. W. Johnson
> Born Jan. 25 1874
> Died Aug. 9 1943
> > (Boggy Bayou Cemetery,
> > Panola County)

Occasionally a brief phrase or line is added to these terse inscriptions, ranging from the ubiquitous "here lies" or "in memory of" to complete sentence epitaphs such as:

> Darling, we miss thee
> > (1909, Bethlehem Cemetery,
> > Collin County)

> She hath done what she could
> > (1917, Chatt Cemetery, Hill
> > County)

> Meet me in Heaven
> > (Union Cemetery, Gustine,
> > Comanche County)

> They were real Texans
> > (Mount Hope Cemetery,
> > Tyler County) [27]

> A Texas Cowboy Comes Home
> > (1977, Voca Cemetery,
> > McCulloch County)

In the folk phase, these modest inscriptions often follow guide lines laboriously scribed in the native stone. Phonetic spelling abounds, and backward letters are common (Figs. 3-8, 3-9).

More Informative Inscriptions

While the typical southern inscription is both brief and rather uninformative, a minority is somewhat lengthier and provides data on migration, kinship, personality or character traits, cause of death, or some other identification beyond mere dates. It is surprising, given the southerner's obsession with genealogy, that the birthplaces of those who migrated to Texas are so rarely recorded on the grave markers. Perhaps the customary silence of the stones concerning origins reflects the American backwoodsman's compulsive mobility, his lack of attachment to place. "It is of no consequence where I was born," the dead southerners seem to say, "for my people moved often and had no roots." The thin scattering of tombstones inscribed with the state or even county of birth is hardly adequate to permit generalizations concerning the specific origins of the local population at large, but they do at least suggest some of the sources and migratory paths. A few such inscriptions are clearly based only in a phonetic recollection of the geography of birth:

> Johnethan Philips
> Was Borned
> Saro. Co. N.C. [Surry?]
> August 1794
> Died Jan 12 1857
> Ag. 62 Ye. 5 Mo.
> > (Williams Cemetery, Collin
> > County)

> Squire Cruse
> Born in Kentucky 1796
> Came to Texas Jan 1834
> Died at Wolf Creek
> Tyler County 1877
> > (Cruse Cemetery, Tyler
> > County)

Others, a tiny minority, are more specific about birth and migration, suggesting the complicated and frequent movements of many southerners who came to Texas:

> W. A. Hardy
> Born in Henrico Co. Va.
> Aug 16, 1807
> Went to Charleston S.C.
> Then to I T in 1818 & in
> 1831 to Ala. then to Miss.
> & Nov. 9 went to Pontotoc
> Co. Miss. emmigrated to
> Tex. Dec. 18, 1882 &
> Died
> May 7, 1890
> > (Old City Cemetery, Paris,
> > Lamar County)

In an East Texas graveyard, one family plot contains an unusual genealogical stone:

> Fuller
> Ancestral Family
> Robert Fuller[1] immigrated 1640–1688
> Jonathan Fuller[2] 1643–1720
> Samuel Fuller[3] 1681–1765
> Benjamin Fuller[4] 1720–1762
> Thaddeus Fuller[5] 1758–1834
> James Fuller[6] 1790–1861
> Aaron Fuller[7] 1821–1909
> Erected by E. Dean Fuller
> > (Concord Cemetery,
> > Harrison County)

A variety of terse eulogizing inscriptions tell something about the personality or character of the dead. "A loving mother" and "a lifelong Baptist" share the ground with a man for whom "honesty was his motto":[28]

> A consistent member
> of the Methodist Church
> for 14 years
> > (Cruse Cemetery, Tyler
> > County)[29]

> As a husband
> devoted; as a father
> affectionate;
> As a friend ever
> kind and true
> > (1900, Whites Chapel
> > Cemetery, Tarrant County)

Kinship, too, is important to the southerner. Frequently, such inscriptions as "wife of" or its older version, "consort of," and "infant son of" appear, or sometimes kinship is the only substantial piece of information presented:

> Johnie
> Adams
> B. Sept th 22 1898
> D. Sept th 27
> 1898
> A Son of
> J. J. Adams
> > (front and back of headstone,
> > Indian Creek Cemetery,
> > Cooke County)

Babe
of
C. C. & M. J. Dial
1867
> (Lonesome Dove Cemetery,
> Tarrant County)

Aunt Bet Littrell
1842–1911
> (Trinity Cemetery, Denton
> County)

The emotional bond that sometimes developed between black and white within the institution of slavery occasionally found expression on tombstones:

Rest in Peace
General
An old negro
Servant.
Property of.
W. K. & S. E.
Pierce
> (Callisburg Cemetery, Cooke
> County)

Some of these inscriptions are longer, attaining the status of true epitaphs. They convey meaningful messages or hopeful explanations to the graveyard visitor:

To live in the hearts
We leave behind
Is not to die
> (1907, Union Cemetery,
> Gustine, Comanche County)

Why should we weep when
the weary ones rest
For death is no more
than a dream
> (Cooper Creek Cemetery,
> Denton County)

He is just a round the
conner little out of
sight
> (1961, cement folk marker,
> Macedonia Cemetery, Brazos
> County)

God needed
two more
angel
children
amidst His
shining
band
> (1899, Macedonia Cemetery,
> Panola County)

But is he dead, no no he
lives. His happy spirit
flies, To Heaven above
and then received, The
long expected prize
> (1915, Trinity Cemetery,
> Denton County)

The Angels called him
> (1876, child, Prairie Grove
> Cemetery, Limestone
> County)

Hopes once bright are now departed,
Since mother's numbered 'mong the dead
> (1892, Whites Chapel
> Cemetery, Tarrant County)

The cause and season of death are sometimes mentioned. Stones may display a plaintive cry that the deceased was "murdered," a lament that "he drowned in Henrietta Creek," or a caustic complaint that "his death was caused by evil friends and lying tongues."[30] Equally pointed is a carefully crafted Denton County sandstone marker:

And. J. Brown
Born
June 17. 1854
Executed
Nov. 21. 1879
> (Old City Cemetery,
> Denton, burial with feet to
> the west)

Sometimes the message is more cryptic. On one Tennessee gravestone is the simple inscription "Jesus called," rendered rather ominous by the presence of a "Princess" telephone, mercifully disconnected, on the adjacent grave mound. A Texas child's death on

Christmas day led the bereaved to rationalize it as:

> A Christmas gift to Heaven
>> (1905, Bolivar Cemetery,
>> Denton County)

Probably the most common juvenile epitaph among Anglo-Texans is the hopeful plea that the child:

> Budded on earth to bloom in Heaven
>> (ubiquitous)

Rhymed Verses

Rhymed verse epitaphs appear infrequently on folk tombstones in Texas, in spite of their antiquity in Britain and the popularity of ballads in the traditional southern music (Fig. 3-15). Epitaphs of this type date at least to the 1600s in Britain and were very common there in the eighteenth century.[31] Among the few in Texas that predate the commercial tombstone era is the famous medieval British–northwestern European rhyme in which the dead one speaks to warn the survivors that they, too, should prepare for death (see box):[32]

> Elizbeth Simpson was borne
> April the 10 1834 and dide
> September 24 1864
> And re member as yo
> ar pasing by yo must
> dy as well as I
>> (cemetery on Shin Oak
>> Ridge, Williamson County)

> Bear in mind as you
> pass by. As you are
> now Once was I. As I
> am now you must be
> Prepare for death,
> And follow me
>> (1889, Chalk Mountain
>> Cemetery, Somervell County)

> Remember friends, as you pass by,
> As you are now, so once was I
> As I am now you soon will be
> prepare for death and follow me
>> (1863, grave on Julian Creek,
>> Bandera County)

SOME BRITISH ANTECEDENTS OF THE ANGLO-TEXAN SPEAKING DEAD EPITAPH

The tomb of Edward, the Black Prince (1330–1376), in Canterbury Cathedral, bears a French epitaph which may be translated as follows:
Such as you are, once was I
Such as I am, such shall you be
This tradition survived over the centuries in Britain, as is exemplified by the following rhymed 1666 epitaph from Perthshire, Scotland:
As. ye. ar. nou
So. onc. vas. Ay
As. Ay. am. so. sal
Ye. be. Remembre
Man. that. thou
Mist. dei

> **—Derived from information in Betty Willsher and Doreen Hunter, *Stones: A Guide to Some Remarkable Eighteenth Century Gravestones*, pp. 21, 121.**

FIG. 3-24. Rhymed verse, together with the heart symbol and stylistic wreath on an infant's grave marker, 1898, Indian Creek Cemetery, Cooke County. The verse reads "A sleep / in Jesus / Blessed sleep / Wheare None / Ever wake / To weep." Photo by the author, 1980.

Stop and read as you pass by
As you are now
Once was I
As I am now
You will be
Prepare for death and follow me
        (1903, Lawhon Springs
        Cemetery, Lee County)

Another verse occasionally appearing on homemade markers is one or another variant of the pragmatic remark that the dead one is asleep (Fig. 3-24):

Asleep in Jesus
Blessed sleep
From which none
Ever awakes to weep
        (Confederate Cemetery,
        Brazoria County)

Rhymed verse epitaphs increased greatly in frequency with the advent of commercially cut markers. Each stonecutter had a copy of a published verse book, and the bereaved chose an appropriate rhyme from among the hundreds listed. In time, the common folk began pirating these, rendering them in phonetic English on their homemade markers:

Here I la mi burdan down
Chang the crows two the crown
        (1900, Bradley Springs
        Cemetery, Shelby County)

Rhymed epitaphs are of several types. Some follow the older folk tradition of the speaking dead, in which the deceased person is made to utter one final message from the beyond (Fig. 3-19):

Farewell my wife and child
From you a father Christ doth call
Mourn not for me, it is vain
To call me to your sight again
        (1891, Bethlehem Cemetery,
        Collin County)

Farewell my wife and children all
From you a father Christ does call
        (Panola County)[33]

Will you come to my
grave when my spirit has
fled, and beneath the cold clay
I am laid with the dead
            (1902, child, Mount Calvary
            Cemetery, Tarrant County)

Weep not, papa and mama for me
For I am waiting in Heaven for thee
            (1923, child, Trinity
            Cemetery, Denton County)

Another type, with roots in the "farewell"
folk inscriptions, allows the survivors to ad-
dress the dead:

On that bright
Immortal shore
We shall meet to
Part no more
            (1922, Chalk Mountain
            Cemetery, Somervell
            County)

It was hard indeed to part with thee,
But Christ's strong arms supported me
            (Panola County)[34]

Rest, mother, rest in
quiet sleep
While friends in sorrow
O'er thee weep
            (1901, Nancy Smith
            Cemetery, Somervell
            County)

Dearest loved one, we have laid thee
In the peaceful grave's embrace
But thy memory will be cherished
Till we see thy heavenly face
            (1895, Mount Zion
            Cemetery, Panola County)

Sleep on sweet babe
and take thy rest
God called thee home
He thought it best
            (Panola County)[35]

Still other rhymed verses permit the bereaved
to speak to anyone who might be interested,
expressing hope, bitterness, or despair:

In love she lived
In peace she died
Her life was craved
But God denied
            (1918, Williams Cemetery,
            Collin County)

A precious one
from us is gone
A voice we lov-
ed is stilled
A place is va-
cant in our home
Which never
can be filled
            (1900, Cowboy Cemetery,
            McCulloch County)

Our father has gone to a
Mansion of rest
To the Glorious land of the
Deity blest
            (1906, Bethlehem Cemetery,
            Collin County)

To them, we trust, a place is given
Among the saints with Christ in Heaven
            (1895, husband and wife,
            Stoney Point Cemetery,
            Collin County)

Another link is
broken in
Our household
band
But a chain
is forming in
a better land
            (1915, Stoney Point
            Cemetery, Collin County)

The tint of health has left her cheek
And cold is her fair brow
Her eyes are closed, her pulse is still
She is an angel now
            (1894, young woman,
            Tomball area, Harris
            County, from a rubbing at
            the Spring Creek County
            Historical Association
            Museum, Tomball)

He was too good,
Too gentle, and fair,
To dwell in this
Cold world of care
          (child, Panola County)[36]

Loved ones have gone from our circle
On earth we shall meet them no more
They have gone to their home in Heaven
And all their affections are o'er.
          (1929, husband and wife,
          Nancy Smith Cemetery,
          Somervell County)

No pain, no grief, no anxious fear,
Can reach the peaceful sleeper here
          (Grayson County)[37]

This marble to Carrie's grave
Is reared by kindred left
Her soul in bliss is now above,
Her friends on earth bereft
          (1892, nineteen-year-old
          woman, Arwine Cemetery,
          Tarrant County)

He took her from a world of care
An everlasting bliss to share
          (1890, child, Cedar Point
          Cemetery, Brown County)

The heyday of epitaphs in the southern cemeteries of Texas occurred in the half-century between about 1880 and 1930. Since then, corresponding to a trend in the American popular culture at large, inscriptions, particularly rhymed verses, have fallen out of fashion.[38] Most commercial and folk stones being erected today represent a reversion to the terse name-and-dates inscriptions of the previous century. In that sense, at least, the southern tradition is being reasserted.

Traditional southern grave markers, then, extend the symbolism rampant in the folk cemetery of the American South. In their form, inscriptions, and epitaphs they speak of distant pagan ancestors and low church British Protestantism, of love and hope, tragedy and despair, of certain doom and faith triumphant. They, together with the other elements of the folk cemetery, unite in death vestiges of the three parent cultures that sired the South—European, African, and Amerindian. One can learn much about Texas from them.

However, you have only to venture into the graveyards of Texas' other ethnic groups to find very different material cultures, reflective of the vivid necrogeographical mosaic. Nowhere will a visual contrast to the traditional southern cemetery strike you more forcefully than in the burial grounds of the Hispanic Texans. Accordingly, Chapter 4 is devoted to the Mexican American cemetery.

The Mexican Graveyard in Texas

4

PERSONS OF Spanish surname now form a quarter or more of the Texas population and seem destined to attain, in the not-too-distant future, a position of numerical equality with the southern Anglos. The state is, as a result, receiving a massive infusion of Hispanic cultural traits, reinforcing a tradition as old as Texas itself. That influence is felt in many facets of life, and no less in death (Fig. 4-1).

Perhaps it is inappropriate to consider the Mexican American traditional cemetery in a single chapter, given the large size and great internal diversity of the group. The framework of cultural unity provided by the Spanish language and Roman Catholicism scarcely conceals fundamental contrasts. Hispanics in the Southwest run the gamut from Castilian to Indian and, consequently, bear a culture that is both varied and regionalized. Even within Texas, noteworthy cultural differences exist between, say, El Paso County's Hispanized Pueblo Indians, whose ancestors came down from New Mexico three centuries ago; the upper-class South Texas Castilian *tejanos*, descended from colonial landgrant families; the middle-class *mestizo* of Central Texas, acculturated through generations of residence as a minority among the Anglos; and the monolingual laborers recently arrived in the *colonias* of the lower Rio Grande Valley.

These distinctive Mexican regional subcultures find expression in religion, architecture, foods, folklore, and many other facets of the Mexican American way of life. The Hispanos of the northern New Mexico highlands, for example, traditionally lived in log dwellings; adobe construction prevailed among their linguistic kinsmen in trans-Pecos West Texas; and stone or palisado walls were the rule in South Texas.

The traditional graveyard, too, bears witness to the Hispanic cultural variety in the Southwest. Highland Hispanos of New Mexico still maintain folk cemeteries very like those of sixteenth-century Iberia (see box), but the graveyards of South and Central Texas *mestizos* apparently reveal more diverse cultural elements, some of which are probably Amerindian in origin. Even so, the cemeteries of Texas' Spanish-speaking peoples have much in common.[1] Many of these burial places, from the headwaters of the Rio Grande to its mouth, share an array of traits and form elements, such as the wooden cross grave marker and elaborate floral decoration (Fig. 4-2). The situation is very like that of the southern folk cemetery, in which whites, blacks, and southeastern Indians more or less share a common funerary material culture. Certainly, the village cemeteries of the Rio Arriba and the Valley have more in common than either does with the traditional Anglo graveyard.[2] In the same sense, then, that we spoke of a "southern" cemetery, we can designate a "Hispanic" or "Mexican" type.

Site and Sanctity

The burial ground of medieval Spain was, in every sense of the word, holy. An ancient Catholic sanctity of cemeteries, reinforced by

FIG. 4-1. The mountains of Old Mexico provide a
fitting background for San Lorenzo Cemetery, situated in a barren pasture on *tierra muerta* above the
fertile Rio Grande Valley in El Paso County. A central cross and saintly name convey the impression
of Catholic sanctity, as do the individual grave
crosses. Photo by the author, 1980.

the religious fervor of the *reconquista*, caused
the Castilian *camposanto*, literally "saint's
field" or "blessed field," to acquire a special
sacredness. Burial was often within the church
structure itself, a practice still common at the
time of Hispanic overseas settlement in the
New World.

These traditions of sanctified cemeteries
and church burial passed intact to the Spanish
colonial frontiers, including eighteenth-century Texas. Human bones have been found
beneath the floors of San Antonio's missions
and the city's San Fernando cathedral. A royal
edict in 1798 forbidding additional burials inside churches, for reasons of public health,
failed to stop the practice, partly because families of wealth and influence regarded church
burial as a status symbol.[3] *Camposantos* were
fine for the poor and for converted Indians,
but not for *ricos*. Even some of the Anglos
who died in the siege of the Alamo were interred in San Antonio churches. At nearby
San José Mission, priests were buried in the
walls of the church, while Christianized Indians found their rest in the *camposanto* in
front of the structure. Even though sanctified,
the early *camposanto* in Texas also served
nonreligious functions. San José's Indian
cemetery, measuring about 220 feet square,
was also the mission's *plaza de armas*, or parade ground.

Many Hispanic graveyards in Texas retain their medieval sanctity yet today, a condition announced by a saintly name and a large public cross, devoid of a crucifix (Fig. 4-3). The Tigua and other Hispanized Indians in the El Paso area seem to have held most rigorously to the sanctified burial ground. At Socorro, one of the El Paso missions, the La Purisema *camposanto* lies in front of the venerable church, visually greeting the faithful as they emerge through the main door. In most of Texas, the accepted date for cemetery maintenance remains November 2, All Souls' Day, reinforcing the concept of sanctity.

In many areas, though, graveyard sanctity has been undermined and greatly diminished by two major causal forces. Anticlericalism, emanating initially from Madrid and later from Mexico City, provided the first of these forces. The disorder associated with the fall of the Spanish Empire and the Texas Revolution made matters worse. As a result the Catholic church in Texas experienced a disastrous decline between about 1790 and 1840. Mission lands underwent secularization and the power of the monastic orders was broken. By the end of the period of decline, many parishes were without priests, and Catholicism survived mainly in a less formal lay folk form. Graveyard sanctity experienced a decline roughly in proportion to that of the organized church. Unsanctified family, community, and rancho *cementarios* apparently came into widespread use during this period and have remained a part of the Texas Hispanic scene ever since (Fig. 4-4).

The second force working to destroy the traditional sanctity of burial grounds has operated mainly since about 1850, and particularly after the turn of the century. Mexican Americans began migrating northward into counties and communities dominated numerically by Anglos, acquiring in the process a minority status. Rather than purchase land for their own cemeteries, they typically requested and received permission to bury their dead in unsanctified Anglo graveyards. To a quite remarkable degree, Hispano and Anglo share burial grounds, both town and rural, through Central and North Texas. Even in a

HISPANO GRAVEYARDS IN NEW MEXICO

Some of the most fascinating and distinctive Hispanic cemeteries in the United States are found in the highland villages of New Mexico, as John R. Stilgoe reports. Such is the conservatism inherent in these places that the graveyard of medieval Christian Spain has been preserved:

"Only in New Spain did the pre-Reformation burying ground survive almost intact. There a tall cross still ordered the sacred enclosure next to the church, and there the old traditions of care took root. Today such graveyards are concentrated in tiny Spanish-American villages in New Mexico. The ancient symbols—the cross, sheep, angels, tree of life, and heart—decorate the hand-carved wooden markers fenced off from grazing cattle. To be sure, the vegetation is different, but the rabbitbrush and tumbleweed cannot hide the eight-foot cross that announces the mysteries of Catholicism. Elsewhere in the United States such graveyards are virtually unknown."

—John R. Stilgoe, "Folklore and Graveyard Design," *Landscape* 22, no. 3 (Summer 1978):27, reprinted with permission.

FIG. 4-2. A small statue of the Madonna and elaborate floral decoration nearly fill the curbing of this Mexican American grave in the Fredericksburg Catholic Cemetery, Gillespie County. Photo by the author, 1977.

FIG. 4-3. The focal point of Our Lady of Perpetual Help Cemetery in New Braunfels is a large wooden cross, as is typical in Mexican graveyards. In the foreground, a statue of the Virgin stands over the grave of a wife and mother. Photo by the author, 1980.

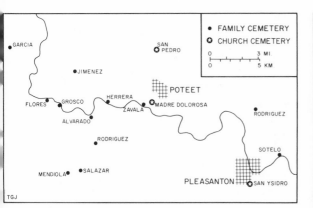

FIG. 4-4. Mexican American cemeteries in the upper Atascosa River Valley, South Texas. Private family graveyards are quite common, and some perhaps date from the *ranchero* period prior to Texas independence. The church cemeteries are, without exception, more recent in origin. Source: United States Geological Survey quadrangle maps, 1 : 24,000.

FIG. 4-5. This marker, atypical because it is made of stone and lists a birthplace in Mexico, stands in a small cluster of Hispanic graves at Cooper Creek Cemetery in dominantly Anglo Denton County. Photo by the author, 1975.

county as purely "hill southern" as Denton, the visitor to rural graveyards will sometimes find, in a corner or adjacent to a fence, a few Spanish-language tombstones—startling and unexpected reminders of the multiple peopling of Texas (Fig. 4-5). At Wrightsboro in Gonzales County, the unsanctified community cemetery now has a sizable Hispanic quarter, partitioned from the Anglo section by a fence and entered through a separate gate (Fig. 4-6). Internally, no gate links the two ethnic clusters. In this manner, the Texas "dual town" has been reflected in miniature. Wrightsboro is not atypical.

In Central Texas, Mexican and German dead also frequently have separate quarters within the same grounds, both in Catholic and in private families cemeteries. At the Kneupper family cemetery in the German-settled hills of Kendall County, for example, the Mexican graves lie just outside the enclosing fence, while at nearby German Catholic St. Joseph's (Honey Creek) in Comal County, two rows of rough wooden crosses marking the Mexican burials occupy one corner of the sanctified enclosure (see Fig. 5-3).

FIG. 4-6. Entrance to the Mexican quarter of the Wrightsboro town cemetery, Gonzales County. Such dual cemeteries are common in South Central Texas. Photo by the author, 1980.

But even when the cemeteries are shared with Anglos or Germans, the Mexicans decorate and maintain their graves in distinctive ways. Sanctity may have been discarded; ethnicity has not.

The sites chosen for *camposantos*, in farming communities at least, often lay on land too poor to till—*tierra muerta*.[4] San Lorenzo Cemetery in rural El Paso County, near Clint, beautifully reflects this preference. Perched on barren *tierra muerta* heights above the irrigated Rio Grande Valley, San Lorenzo offers a fine view across the lush plains to distant mountains in Old Mexico (Fig. 4-1).

Internal Pattern

Hispanos, so obedient to the compass when laying out the street plans of their orderly colonial towns, seem to have ignored it in their burial grounds. An almost haphazard spatial arrangement of the dead is typical, and no point of the compass enjoys special significance in the placement of graves. Perhaps this disorder in death reflects the unplanned pattern of the traditional Mexican village, with its Indian roots, so that graveyard and village alike remained conservative refuges from the geometry of the *conquistadores*.

East offers no magic to the Mexican *muertos*, in contrast to its monumental importance to the southerner. Nor are graves within the same cemetery normally oriented in a uniform manner. Two, three, or even more axes may be used in a burial ground, producing a pattern chaotic and vaguely discomforting to the Anglo eye (Fig. 4-7). At Wrightsboro, the majority of Mexican burials are feet-to-south, while across the fence in the Anglo quarter the ancient directional devotion to the rising sun and holy city is evident. Similarly, at San Elizario in El Paso County, the most common burial orientation is feet-to-north, but many face the south and some the east. Even within one family plot at San Elizario, four burials are on a north-south axis and one east-west, permitting a fuller utilization of the limited space. Occasionally, graves are positioned so as to face the cemetery's central cross.

This lack of consistent burial orientation in Texas duplicates the situation in Spain, where various layouts occur. Often, particularly in the churchyards of northern and northwestern Spain, the feet of the dead point toward the church building. Less commonly in Spain, orientation is to the cemetery gate, to the east, or away from the village. Priests typically rest in the opposite direction than the secular dead, in order to face their parishioners in the afterworld.[5]

The prevalent spatial pattern within the Mexican cemetery serves to emphasize the individual grave rather than husband-wife or clan groupings, an effect heightened visually by curbing or fencing around each burial. In Central and South Texas, cement curbing is the rule, but the *indios* and *hispanos* of the El Paso area, as well as certain other parts of Texas and New Mexico, prefer wooden picket fences, or *cerquitas*.[6] Both techniques draw the visitor's eye (Figs. 4-8, 4-25).

Scholars studying the *camposantos* of highland New Mexico attribute the *cerquita* to Anglo influence, suggesting that the local *hispanos* were attempting to copy the commercial cast-iron grave fences introduced in the late nineteenth century (see Fig. 2-25).[7] A parallel adoption may have occurred in Texas. However, Theodore Gentilz' and Stephen Seymour Thomas' nineteenth-century paintings of San José mission in San Antonio appear to show several *cerquitas* in the old *camposanto* in front of the church.[8] The rarity of the custom among Anglos, coupled with its widespread occurrence among Hispanics, lead me to doubt that the *cerquitas* were borrowed.

Emphasis on the individual is heightened by the presence of elongated grave mounds, essentially identical to those of the southerners. Mounds are most common, or even dominant, along the Rio Grande in far West Texas, where curbing is rare, but they also appear with regularity in central and southern parts of the state (Fig. 4-9). In the Big Bend country, represented by Terlingua in Brewster County, sizable flat slabs of rock cover the mounds, perhaps to discourage desecration by wild animals (Fig. 4-10).

FIG. 4-7. The Mexican quarter of the community cemetery at Wrightsboro in Gonzales County is equipped with a roofed shed containing discarded church pews for visitors. Note the use of crosses and lack of consistent compass orientation of the graves. Photo by the author, 1980.

FIG. 4-8. A grave enclosed by a wooden picket *cerquita* at San Elizario in El Paso County. Such fences are common in the Mexican cemeteries of far West Texas, as is the wooden cross. The grave is in the children's sector of the cemetery, and the marker bears no inscription. Photo by the author, 1980.

FIG. 4-9. A bare earth mound in the grassless Ysleta cemetery, El Paso County. The simple wooden cross, painted white with a black inscription, is found in most Mexican American graveyards. Photo by the author, 1980.

A MEXICAN CEMETERY IN CENTRAL TEXAS, ABOUT 1940

"There is a cemetery in the outskirts of Austin . . . where every mound tells a readable story of the person buried beneath it. Here is a small grave and scattered across its top a doll, a bicycle bell, a tiny spoon, a dish, and a bag of vari-colored marbles. Here a larger spot covered with razor and brush, and a rusty watch. And still another with a woman's comb, a few articles or wearing apparel, toilet articles, bracelets, and beads. Mound after mound—it is like walking through some fantastic market place. No one seems to know just where the idea had its beginning among the Mexicans in that section of the country but the belief is that it was borrowed from the Indians."

> —Dorothy Jean Michael, quoting C. L. Douglas in "Grave Decoration," *Backwoods to Border*, Publications of the Texas Folklore Society, no. 18, 1943, p. 135; reprinted with permission.

The typically southern preference for husband-to-right burial is not evident in the Hispanic cemetery, nor does the family plot enjoy much importance. Occasionally, as at San Elizario, one sees such signs as "Familia Arias" posted in small plots, but even there a separate children's section exists (Fig. 4-11). In this sense, the traditional graveyard fails to reflect the strong, patriarchal Mexican family.

This is not to imply that the Hispano-Texas cemetery lacks a focal point. Normally, even in unsanctified burial grounds, the large central cross serves that function.[9] In at least one graveyard, a small pavilion, somewhat similar in appearance to the bandstands found in Mexican town plazas, occupies the central

FIG. 4-10. Large flat slabs of rock cover Mexican grave mounds at Terlingua in Brewster County. The slabs may be intended to discourage scavenging wild animals. Note the intrusion by native shrubs and cacti. Photo courtesy of Professor Francis E. Abernethy of Stephen F. Austin State University, Nacogdoches, Texas.

position (Fig. 4-7). Equipped with benches for visitors, the pavilion offers shade from the summer sun and a place to sit.

The Mexican cemetery, like its counterpart in the American South, normally is fenced. These enclosures vary from massive mortared stone walls, as at Ysleta, to simple barbed-wire pasture fences. Apparently, the origin of the custom is Castilian, since the graveyards of Spanish villages in the New Mexican highlands and of Castile itself are also "almost invariably walled" or fenced.[10] The British-American lichgate, by contrast, is rarely present, and where it does occur, acculturation is the most likely explanation (Fig. 1-3).

Vegetation and Plantings

Mexican Americans appear little concerned
with introduced permanent shrub and tree
plantings (Fig. 4-1). Junipers, crape myrtles,
roses, and the other exotic bushes typical of
traditional southern cemeteries are generally
absent. Native vegetation and volunteers,
such as salt cedars, mesquite, greasewood,
and cacti, are usually tolerated rather than removed (Fig. 4-10). Rarely are these or any
other shrubs deliberately planted, though I did
see cactus carefully placed on one grave
mound at the La Purisema *camposanto* in Socorro. No doubt the semiaridity of the Hispanic counties helps explain the inattention
to cemetery bushes and shrubbery, but a traditional Amerindian desire for harmony with
Nature may provide part of the answer.

The lack of formal cemetery shrubs and
bushes is more than offset by highly elaborate
floral decoration (Fig. 4-2). "Natural flowers,
both wild and cultivated, grow profusely in
the spring and early summer," and the entire
grave mound or space within the grave curbing is typically covered or filled with cut,
plastic, paper, or potted flowers.[11] Colorful
wreaths are often tied to the wooden or cement crosses (Fig. 4-12). Perhaps the traditional Mexican custom of making paper
flowers conditioned them to adopt more readily the durable plastic variety, but in any case
all types of artificial flower are more common
in their graveyards than in the burial decoration of other ethnic groups. The overall visual
impact is that of a flower garden or florist's
shop. Elaborate funerary floral decoration, as
practiced by the Mexican Texans, may have
ancient roots in the Mediterranean region,
but the artistic use of flowers is also indigenous to Mexico and, in the modern cemetery,
likely reflects Indian origin.

A great many, perhaps the majority of, traditional Mexican cemeteries in Texas, as well
as New Mexico, lack grass (Fig. 4-9). In a desert setting, this absence is not unexpected,
and some medieval graveyards in semiarid
portions of New Castile probably had a similar appearance. When grass or weeds do

FIG. 4-11. A fine rustic wooden cross, homemade,
stands in a Mexican family plot at San Elizario
cemetery in El Paso County. Note the use of white-
wash, both on the cross and on the tree trunk, and
the hand-lettered inscription in black. Plastic
flowers decorate the marker. What appears to be a
sun symbol adorns the cross. Photo by the author,
1980.

sprout, Hispanos typically remove them, much in the manner of East Texas Anglos, blacks, and Indians (Fig. 2-2).[12] On a Saturday in mid-September, I once watched a group of men at Socorro remove the summer's accumulation of weeds using hoes and a tractor, undeterred by a wedding in progress at adjacent La Purisema mission. Clearly, more than semiaridity is at work in retarding the growth of grass and weeds. The same Muslim Saharan graveyard barrenness that may have reached the American South by way of the African slave coast also could have spread to Texas through Moorish Spain and Mexico (Fig. 2-5). The weed choppers I saw that autumn day at Socorro perhaps obeyed their vestigial Moorishness. If so, it would not be the only example of Arabic influence to be found in the Mexican cemetery.

FIG. 4-12. Tacks driven into a whitewashed wooden cross spell out the name of the deceased at San Lorenzo Cemetery in El Paso County. Plastic flowers are tied to the cross. Photo by the author, 1980.

Grave Markers

In frontier times, most graves in the Spanish settlements had no markers at all. The priest made an entry in the Libro de Enterros ("Book of Burials") kept at each church, describing the spot of burial, using terms such as "the gospel side of the sanctuary rail" or simply "in the *camposanto*."[13] Rich and poor, Spaniard and Indian alike received such treatment. The lack of markers is suggested by the practice, previously mentioned, of using the *camposanto* at Mission San José as the Indians' parade ground.

After about 1820, tombstones became more common. Some scholars believe that Mexican American grave markers represent a borrowing from Anglo culture, since colonial Hispanic prototypes are virtually nonexistent and the first use of markers coincides with early Anglo penetrations of the Southwest.[14] The abundance of grave markers in Spain and Mexico seems to refute this claim, as does the fundamental difference in shape and appearance between Anglo and Mexican memorials.

Once the custom began spreading, wood became the preferred material for Mexican grave markers in Texas, duplicating the Old World Spanish preference, and in some districts it remains dominant still today (Fig. 4-13).[15] The explanation for this preference could lie in the rarity of wood in semiarid districts, coupled with a desire to fashion the memorial out of something rare and precious. In more recent times, the opposite argument could also be made, since wood, being relatively cheap, could be regarded as an index of poverty. Whatever the reason, wood was and is widely preferred. Its perishability, combined with the colonial custom of unmarked graves, mean that no Hispanic markers of considerable age can be found. I know of none in Texas over a century old.

The only serious challenge to wood as a material is provided by commercial cement, a product of the industrial age and popular culture (Fig. 4-14). Mexican cement markers do retain some measure of folk or traditional culture because they are manufactured singly, by local craftsmen working at home. The widespread acceptance of cement markers by Mexican Americans in Texas began in the 1920s and has spread to all parts of the state.

Wrought or cast iron and other metal grave markers constitute a persistent, if small, minority in Mexican cemeteries, as in Spain (Fig. 4-15).[16] They may often be status symbols associated with the upper class, though some recent specimens were manufactured

from scrap metal in garage workshops (Fig. 4-16). Mexicans in Texas seldom use native rock to produce *lápidas*, or tombstones, in spite of the well-known Hispanic stoneworking abilities and the presence of fine stone markers in highland New Mexico hispano cemeteries.[17] Looking at the intricate and beautiful carved stones on the San José mission in San Antonio, one can only be puzzled and disappointed that these skilled craftsmen did not turn their attention to funerary art.

FIG. 4-13. The wooden "cross within cross" is a typically Mexican repetition, as here at San Elizario in El Paso County. An inscription, now partially illegible, is carved into the main cross, both above and below the smaller cross. Photo by the author, 1980.

FIG. 4-14. Five hearts adorn the 1929 cement grave marker of a baby in the Panteón Hidalgo, New Braunfels. The lower part of the cross bears the impressions of fern leaves. A coat of pastel pink paint covers the marker. The meaning of the cryptic abbreviation d.e.r.s.p.d.c.b.y. . . . is unclear, but the first part may stand for *dedican este recuerdo sus padres* . . . Photo by the author, 1980.

Tombstones have become more common with the progress of acculturation and the advent of popular culture, but traditional examples are rare (Fig. 4-5).

The preferred and almost universal shape of Mexican and Old World Spanish grave markers, regardless of material composition, is the Latin cross.[18] In wood, these crosses reveal a variety of common subtypes, differing in the precise configuration of the three exposed ends (Fig. 4-17). Some are crudely formed of

FIG. 4-15. A baby's grave bears an attractive wrought-iron marker at Ysleta in El Paso County. The inscription says simply "Niña C S" ["little girl C S"]. Photo by the author, 1980.

FIG. 4-16. A simple homemade iron cross marks a grave in the Mexican section of the Catholic cemetery at Fredericksburg. Note the shells lying loosely at the base of the cross and the potted flowers. Photo by the author, 1977.

FIG. 4-17. Some common generic subtypes of wooden Latin crosses found on Mexican graves in Texas. Specific observations: 1-3, Ysleta, El Paso County; 4, 9, 12, Terlingua, Brewster County; 5, Calvary Cemetery, rural Tarrant County; 6, La Paloma, Cameron County; 7, 9, 10, San Elizario, El Paso County; 8, 11, San Lorenzo, rural El Paso County. The dimensions have been standardized for this illustration.

rough-hewn beams, while others reveal delicate, carefully shaped curves and points. Cement crosses normally display the simple square-ended bars, while wrought-iron markers are the most intricate.

A minority of traditional Mexican American grave markers take some form other than the Latin cross. Perhaps most interesting and common among these are homemade, oblong slabs bearing a bas relief image of the Virgin of Guadalupe, often painted in lifelike colors. The bas relief always appears on the side of the slab facing the burial, lending the grave the appearance of a small shrine. One of the finest bas relief Madonna markers in Texas adorns the grave of Señora Juliana Gonzalez de Villarreal in Our Lady of Perpetual Help Cemetery at New Braunfels (Fig. 4-18). Dating from 1937, this molded cement marker bears

a coat of shining silver paint and is still carefully maintained by descendants of the deceased. It is a joy to behold, particularly on a sunny day.

The marker often shares dominion over the grave with a miniature shrine or small reliquary, similar to those seen in the yards of Mexican homes (Fig. 4-19). Perhaps we might best refer to these as *relicaritos*, though no term seems to be in general usage among the Mexican population of Texas. An effigy of the Virgin, a tiny crucifix, a candle, or some icon is placed within these little reliquaries. In shape, some *relicaritos* are reminiscent of Pueblo Indian bake ovens and are in fact called *hornitos* ("little ovens"), while certain others are cylindrical (Fig. 4-20). If no *relicarito* is present, a small *nicho*, usually glass covered, is often recessed into the grave

FIG. 4-18. Made by a local craftsman, this star-be-decked cement bas relief of the Virgin of Guadalupe was erected in 1937 in Our Lady of Perpetual Help Cemetery, New Braunfels. The entire monument is painted silver. It is anything but the *humilde recuerdo* claimed in the epitaph; instead, it ranks as one of the finest vernacular markers in Texas. The inscriptions read "la Señora Juliana Gonzalez de Villarreal Fallecio a la edad de 64 años el 7 de Marzo de 1937—Este humilde recuerdo la dedican su esposo e hijos" and "te salve Maria, llena eres de gracias." ["Mrs. Juliana Gonzalez de Villarreal Died at the age of 64 years on the 7th of March 1937—This humble memorial dedicated to her by her husband and sons"; "Mary, full of grace, save you"]. Photo by the author, 1980.

marker (Figs. 4-21, 4-22). A photograph of the deceased or a saint's image appears in the hollow, along with a crucifix (Fig. 4-23). When neither *relicarito* nor *nicho* is provided, their place is occasionally taken by an open-air, freestanding statue of the Virgin or by a holy image painted on the marker (Fig. 4-24). More recent markers often feature ceramic-tile holy images. On one Bandera County grave mound stands a stone mermaid, *la sirena*, heaped with plastic flowers.[19]

Decoration of the grave marker is accomplished with paint.[20] Whether wooden or cement, the marker acquires a coat of one or another favored hue, such as white, pink, light green, sky blue, or red-orange. Indeed, color is the hallmark of the Hispanic cemetery. To an Anglo, accustomed to the bland, subdued hues of native stone and the somber

FIG. 4-19. A homemade shell-encrusted, cement *relicarito* filled with icons in the rural San José Cemetery, Kerr County. This represents one of the distinctive ways Mexican Americans use shells in grave decoration. Photo by the author, 1979.

FIG. 4-20. Oven-shaped *relicaritos*, or *hornitos*, in the cemetery at Terlingua, Brewster County. Note also the wooden crosses. Photo courtesy of Professor Francis E. Abernethy of Stephen F. Austin State University, Nacogdoches, Texas.

grays of weathered wood or imported marble, the Hispanic grave markers are radically different, even startling. Death, with its Germanic blacks and purples, finds no suggestion in the gaily painted Mexican memorials and abundant flowers. Instead, the graveyard's "flourish of color" seems to be a reaffirmation of life.[21] Such use of color in a sacred context has ample pre-Columbian precedent in Mexico, where even the huge pyramids once bore bright paints.

The riot of color produced by paint and flowers is reinforced and heightened with tiling. A millennium ago Moors taught Iberians to decorate with colored tiles, forming abstract mosaics, and their legacy is abundantly revealed in the Mexican cemeteries of Texas. On the graves of the poor, broken and whole ceramic tiles—red, blue, yellow, white, and green—are pressed into the cement crosses, forming brilliant patterns (Fig. 4-25). The diminutive 1955 Rosa Cantu marker in New Braunfels offers one of the finest examples of the tiled cement cross in Texas. Its craftsman combined bright red, yellow, white, and dark blue tile fragments with black grouting to achieve a memorable visual effect, a distinctively Hispanic beauty found only in folk and primitive art. Abstract designs and checkerboards that would delight the soul of a devout, image-hating Muslim greet the eye from every quarter of some Mexican grave-

FIG. 4-21. A dark-eyed Hispanic Madonna occupies a glassed *nicho* in a tombstone at San Elizario in El Paso County. Photo by the author, 1980.

FIG. 4-22. An image of Christ in a *nicho* at San Elizario in El Paso County. Photo by the author, 1980.

yards. Catholicism prevails on some other memorials, when whole tiles, carefully arranged in the shape of a cross, produce the "cross within cross" often found in older wooden folk markers (Fig. 4-13).

The regional concentration of tile decoration in Texas is greatest in the San Antonio area, extending to nearby county seats. One craftsman, Guadalupe Ybarra, was responsible for many of the tile-covered crosses in and around San Antonio.[22] A first-generation Texan of Mexican-born parentage, Ybarra used his garage and backyard in San Antonio as a workshop. He made no claim to originality in his work, choosing instead to copy "what was already in the local cemeteries and following the wishes of his customers."[23] Ybarra always had a large supply of tiles on hand, both whole and broken.

The American popular culture has provided a variety of other colorful, mass-produced items that find a place in Mexican grave decoration. Pressed into the moist cement of markers and curbings are glass marbles, small plastic crucifixes, bracelet charms, and sundry other trinkets. At San José Cemetery, in Kerr County near Comfort, one grave has marbles arranged in the shape of a cross, and the curbing of another grave there contains tiny plastic bracelet charms in the shape of a boot and a pistol. A rosary sometimes is draped over the top bar of the cross.

FIG. 4-23. A framed photograph of the deceased, to-
gether with some flowers, occupy a glassed *nicho* in
Our Lady of Perpetual Help Cemetery at New
Braunfels. Photo by the author, 1980.

FIG. 4-24. Christ painted on a tombstone in the
Mexican quarter of the Catholic cemetery at Fredericksburg in Gillespie County. Photo by the author,
1977.

FIG. 4-25. A cement Latin cross covered with ceramic tile fragments, dating from 1931, in Our Lady of Perpetual Help Cemetery, New Braunfels. Note also the flowers and grave curbing. Photo by the author, 1980.

MEXICAN GRAVES IN TEXAS

"The grave is usually marked by a handmade concrete cross or other headstone and is bordered by a concrete curbing. Into the concrete of both the cross and the curbing have been set many kinds of decorative items: marbles, costume jewelry, broken crockery, colored tiles, and seashells. The color and originality of these . . . grave decorations is striking. I have seen them in the cemeteries and *panteóns* of Austin, New Braunfels, Houston, and Brownsville, and of Matamoros across the river in Mexico."

—Sara Clark, "The Decoration of Graves in Central Texas with Seashells," in *Diamond Bessie and the Shepherds*, Publications of the Texas Folklore Society, No. 36, p. 34; © Texas Folklore Society; reprinted with permission.

Decorative Symbols

Often carved into the wooden crosses or scratched on the cement markers is one or another of several traditional decorative symbols, some of which are similar to those encountered on southern Anglo stones. Most common is the miniature cross, often repeated two or more times (Fig. 4-18). Also favored is the ascending dove, a symbol found on Hispanic grave markers across much of the Southwest.[24] In Polly's Cemetery, Bandera County, abundant doves, "many of which are charmingly hand-carved," can be seen.[25] Particularly beautiful there is the carving on the marker of Virginia Herrera, dated 1888, com-

bining multiple doves with a delicate Spanish script. In the San Elizario cemetery in El Paso County, a sky-blue 1980 wooden cross, almost a century newer than the Herrera marker, bears a carefully carved dove on the upper bar, evidence that the traditional symbol remains vital today (Fig. 4-26). Presumably, the Hispanic funerary dove carries the same Christian Holy Spirit or ascending-soul meaning as among southern Protestants. In all probability, though, it also has more ancient, long-forgotten ties to the Mediterranean love/mother goddess. I feel certain that the death dove reached Hispanic Texas by way of Spain and Mexico.

Somewhat less common, but still wide-spread, is the heart symbol, carved into the four bars of the cross marker or attached to the cross (Fig. 4-14).[26] At one Mexican grave in the town cemetery in Comfort, a jigsawn heart is affixed at the point where the two bars of the wooden cross meet. Were this symbol not also found among the highland Hispanos of New Mexico, I would be tempted to believe that the Mexicans of Central Texas had adopted the heart motif from the Germans (see Chapter 5).[27] At the very least, it is possible that Mexicans of the San Antonio area copied the distinctively German "turnip-shaped" heart (compare Figs. 4-14 and 5-27).

More common, and also paralleling southern and Texas German custom, is the Mexican use of shells as grave decoration (Fig. 2-10).[28] Shells of different types are employed in "an astounding variety of ways" by Hispanic Texans. Some are pressed into the cement cross or its base, others become part of the cement curbing, and still others rest loosely on the earth or the cross (Fig. 4-16). *Relicaritos* sometimes bear an encrustation of shells (Fig. 4-19). The initials or name of the dead are often spelled out with small shells or a cross is formed with them.[29] A wide range of shells, marine, riverine, and terrestrial alike,

is used, including conches, whelks, snails, oysters, clams, mussels, and cockles.

If questioned about the graveyard shells, Mexicans normally say they are "simply decorations," have "no special meaning," and are used "because they are pretty." Inquiries, coming from an Anglo, often appear to make the Hispano nervous. A few, however, give responses that appear to attach a magico-religious significance to shells. The shell, according to one Mexico City resident, is "the grave of God," and individual Mexican Texans claim that "each shell was contributed by one of the mourners"; that "people found shells at the beach and saved them until a friend or relative died"; and that shells were gathered from a river "to put on each grave after the deaths occurred."[30] When coupled with the fact that shells appear in churchyard *calvarios* ("shrines") and *capillas* ("chapels") in Texas, Mexico, and Spain, as well as in front-yard shrines, these statements leave little doubt that the Hispanic funerary shell is more than mere decoration.

The most tempting explanation for the custom is to conclude that the ancient Mediterranean practice of placing shells on graves also reached Texas by way of Spain and Mexico; in short, that the eternal Magna Mater also survives in the Mexican cemetery. At Compostella in northwestern Spain, one of the most important Christian pilgrimage sites of the Middle Ages, the shell became a symbol of St. James and the Virgin Mary, commemorating the reputed restoration of life to a drowned man. Pilgrims bound for Compostella displayed the shell as their badge.[31] The Virgin-shell association in Spain seems to be a direct survival of the more ancient mother goddess–shell symbolism. If we accept this diffusion and the ancient symbolism that it implies, then some South Texas grave markers, containing the gynosymbolic conch neatly inserted on the potentially phallic top bar of the cross, acquire a most explicit sexual meaning (Fig. 4-27). Bible Belters might even demand that they be "X-rated."

The Iberian-origin, mother-goddess explanation is not, however, without problems. Sara Clark, the leading expert on the subject,

FIG. 4-26. Ascending dove, based on a rubbing made in San Elizario Cemetery, El Paso County. The dove is carved into the top bar of a wooden cross erected in 1980. Sky blue paint adorns the cross, and the lines of figure are black. The dove is a persistent symbol in Mexican American funerary folk art and probably represents the soul winging heavenward.

has traveled extensively in Mexico and, in a recent conversation, told me she has *never* seen funerary shell decoration except in border towns, such as Matamoros and Nuevo Laredo. Some of her informants claim to have encountered the practice at unspecified locales within Mexico, but the custom does not appear to be at all common in that nation. The rarity of shell decoration in Mexico also endangers a possible link to African slaves who were introduced by the Spaniards in colonial times. Still, a systematic search of traditional cemeteries in Mexico has not yet been made. Until and unless it is, the matter of diffusion through Mexico cannot be resolved.

In any case, the possibility of shell decoration having been passed from Anglo to Mexican in the process of acculturation appears

FIG. 4-27. A conch shell is neatly inserted on the top bar of a wooden grave cross at La Paloma Cemetery, Cameron County, Lower Rio Grande Valley. This arrangement may unconsciously perpetuate an ancient sexual/rebirth motif linked to the Mediterranean mother goddess, in which the shell is the symbol of the female and the upright grave marker is phallic. Photo by the author, 1975.

remote. As Sara Clark has noted, the two groups employ fundamentally different types of shell decoration, and the *mestizo* Mexicans in Texas use shells in other, nonfunerary yet clearly religious ways, particularly in *calvarios*.[32]

Further complicating the matter is the regional variation of Hispanic shell decoration within Texas. The custom appears to be strongest in the coastal region, extending inland to the Hill Country and Laredo. In El Paso County, at the western extremity of the state, I found in inspecting several thousand traditional *indio* and *mestizo* graves only *one* instance of shell decoration—a small whelk embedded in the upper bar of a cement cross erected in 1956 at San Elizario. Moreover, the custom seems to be practiced only by the poor class of *mestizos*. Persons of purer Spanish blood, Indians, and middle-class *mestizos* are generally unfamiliar with shell decoration.

Perhaps a clue to the origin comes from Presidio County in far West Texas. There, in a Mexican cemetery on the Rio Grande in the shadow of the Chinati Mountains, each grave is covered with small rocks. According to local tradition, every mourner at the funeral places one rock on the bare grave mound.[33]

Inscriptions

A collector of tombstone inscriptions will be disappointed by the Hispanic Texan cemeteries, for the true epitaph has no place in Mexican folk tradition. Many markers contain no written information at all, reflecting a peasant illiteracy that led words to be subordinate to symbols and designs. Rhymed verse epitaphs are altogether lacking. The cross, shell, and dove bear a very real death magic for the Mexican poor; words and poetry do not.

When inscriptions appear, their purpose is to convey the most basic biographical information, to affirm the strong family ties that characterize Mexican society, or to request rest and salvation for the deceased. So uniform are these terse messages that they become essentially predictable. A few examples will suffice to describe the generic type:

Señorita
Fernandita V. Lopez
Nacio. el. dia. 11 de. May
o. de. 1891. Fallecio. Ener
o. 1. 1913. En. Paz. Descansa
Rdo. de. su. hemo. Jose V. Lopez
[Miss Fernandita V. Lopez
Born. the. 11th. day. of. Ma
y. 1891. Died. Januar
y. 1. 1913. Rest. in. Peace
Rem[embered]. by. her. bro[ther]. Jose V.
     Lopez]
               (Our Lady of Mount Carmel
               Cemetery, Ysleta, El Paso
               County; see Fig. 4-29)

Aqui. descansan. los. restos.
de. German. Martinez. Nacio.
el. año. de. 1904. y. Fallecio.
El. 1915.
[Here. rest. the. remains.
of. German. Martinez. Born.
in. the. year. 1904. and. Died
in. 1915.]
               (Comfort, Kendall County)

Tiburcio Menchaca
Fallesio el 3 de
Julio de 1920
a los 36 anos
de edad
Este es un
recuerdo de su
esposa
Concepsion G.
Menchaca
Denton, Texas
[Tiburcio Menchaca
Died the 3rd of
July in 1920
at 36 years
of age
This is a
memorial by his
wife
Concepsion G.
Menchaca
Denton, Texas]
               (Cooper Creek Cemetery,
               Denton County)

Descansa en Paz
Ramon Puente Perez
Nacio 9-15-1906
Fallecio 5-8-1956
Tu esposa. Tus
hijos. tu padre
y tu hermano
Jamás te Olvitan
[Rest in Peace
Ramon Puente Perez
Born 9-15-1906
Died 5-8-1956
Your wife. Your
sons. your father
and your brother
never forget you]
               (Our Lady of Perpetual Help
               Cemetery, New Braunfels,
               Comal County)

In the majority of such inscriptions, the
biographical data are followed by a phrase
containing the words *recuerdo de* ("remembered by"), *este recuerdo* ("this memorial"),
este humilde recuerdo ("this humble memorial"), or the like, and finally by the names of
various surviving kinfolk. Normally, the kin
remain anonymous:

     recuerdo de sus padres
     [remembered by his parents]
               (1956, Ysleta, El Paso
               County)

     recuerdo de su
     esposa y su hijo
     E. P. D.
     [remembered by his
     wife and his son
     R. I. P.]
               (1956, La Paloma Cemetery,
               Cameron County)

     Recerdos. de. su
     Madre. y. Hermanos
     [Remembered. by. his
     Mother. and. Brothers]
               (1978, Panteón Hidalgo,
               New Braunfels, Comal
               County)

Su esposa e hijos
dedican este recuerdo.
[His wife and sons
dedicate this memorial]
    (1920, Fredericksburg St.
    Mary's Catholic Cemetery,
    Gillespie County)

But sometimes the bereaved are named:

Recuerdo de su
Hija Jovita Sandoval
y Nietas
[Remembered by his
daughter Jovita Sandoval
and granddaughters]
    (1945, San Lorenzo
    Cemetery, El Paso County)

Recuerdo De
A. Guerra
[Remembered by
A. Guerra]
    (1942, Ysleta, El Paso
    County)

Recuerdos de su hijo Miguel
[Remembered by her son Miguel]
    (Socorro, El Paso County)

Recuerdo de su hija Rita
Esposo y Familia
[Remembered by her daughter Rita
Husband and Family]
    (1974, San Elizario, El Paso
    County)

Occasionally a few extra words may appear, usually short statements or supplications, such as *aqui descansa* ("here rests") or *te salve Maria* ("may Mary save you") (Fig. 4-18). Only very rarely is a birthplace in Mexico noted, perhaps partly because of the traffic in illegal aliens (Fig. 4-5).

Of greater interest than the meager inscriptions are the various methods employed to form the words. On traditional wooden crosses, letters are laboriously carved into the surface, sometimes so thickly as to cover all four arms and use every bit of available space (Fig. 6-5). Black paint is carefully applied to the recessed letters, producing a clear contrast

to the lighter color chosen for the rest of the cross (Fig. 4-28). Less durable but also common are inscriptions simply painted onto the flat wood surface, without benefit of carving (Figs. 4-9, 4-11). Still other crosses bear inscriptions spelled out with tacks driven into the wood (Fig. 4-12).

Quite striking, and distinctively Hispanic, is a minority consisting of flat metal inscription plates on which the words appear as stencil-like perforations. The finest perforated

FIG. 4-28. A whitewashed cement marker covered with inscriptions, Ysleta, El Paso County. Many wooden markers are similarly inscribed. Photo by the author, 1980.

FIG. 4-29. The Lopez stenciled metal epitaph plate, Ysleta, El Paso County. For a transcription and translation, see the text. Photo by the author, 1980.

metal marker I have encountered in Texas stands on the grave of Fernandita Lopez at Ysleta in El Paso County (Fig. 4-29). Rusted with age on its metal bar cross, the seventy-year-old Lopez plate still exhibits a dignified beauty. Its folk inscription, increasingly crowded and abbreviated toward the end, argues convincingly for "planning ahead."

The custom of carving or recessing inscriptions passed over into the era of cement markers. Words are either scribed with a stylus into the damp cement or carefully pressed, letter by letter, using manufactured type. Since the cement cross is often covered with tile, preventing lettering, the base is broadened and flared to serve as a tablet for the inscription (Figs. 4-14, 4-25).

Conclusion

Hispanic graveyards are places of color, where paints, flowers, and tiles combine to comfort the bereaved and startle the *gringo*. They, like the folk cemeteries of the American South,

link African, European, and Amerindian influences, for the Iberian Catholic, Moorish Muslim, animistic *indio*, and possibly even the enslaved African have contributed form elements. To comprehend the diverse material content of these burial grounds is to understand the forced marriages of cultures that produced them. The Mexican cemetery represents the last major viable stronghold of the homemade artifact and folk custom in Texas, a virtue that perhaps owes more to poverty than to loyalty to tradition. Popular culture has intruded here but not yet conquered.

To move abruptly from Mexican American to German American may seem a quantum leap. Yet Latino and Teuton have shared Central Texas, particularly the Hill Country, for almost a century and a half, usually occupying the same ranches, towns, and, as we have seen, even cemeteries. In the process, as Chapter 5 will reveal, they have kept their respective funerary cultures largely separate.

The Texas German Graveyard

IN A BROAD, fragmented belt across south-central Texas and in small ethnic islands strewn over much of the remainder of the state live Texans of German descent. Their ancestors immigrated mainly between 1830 and 1890, and by the turn of the century German Americans numbered about 200,000 in the state, constituting roughly 8 percent of the white population and forming the largest ethnic group derived directly from Europe.[1] The cultural imprint of these Germans remains clearly discernible in modern Texas, and their distinctive architecture, customs, dialects, work ethic, and foodways are still much in evidence. Perhaps nowhere is that imprint more vivid (and less researched) than in their traditional graveyards (Fig. 5-1). In no other part of the United States, or for that matter of Germany itself, have I seen grave markers so beautifully expressive of German folk culture. Certainly Texas German funerary art far outshines that of the more heralded Pennsylvania "Dutch."[2]

In the rural and small-town graveyards of south-central Texas, one finds a wide variety of cultural elements—the abundant use of the mother tongue, including some noteworthy indigenous German verse; the craftsmanship of skilled carvers and metalworkers; medieval hex signs and folk art motifs; and typically Teutonic attention to order, neatness, and geometry. Also readily apparent in the graveyards is the diversity of the Texas Germans. They come from many provinces and countless villages, bearing quite different religious and cultural heritages. In Texas about three-fifths of the Christians of German ancestry are Lutheran, one-fourth Roman Catholic, 5 percent Methodist, and another 5 percent Reformed (United Church of Christ), with a scattering of Mennonites, Baptists, and other groups. A small minority of Texas Germans perpetuate a long heritage of agnosticism. The graveyards of the Germans, while reflecting the underlying ethnic identity rooted in language, also reveal the internal divisions along sectarian lines.

Site and Sanctity

In common with Hispanos, the Germans had an Old World heritage of burial in sanctified ground. Throughout rural Germany, as in most of Europe, cemeteries often occupy the yard surrounding the church building, a location implied in the word *Kirchhof*. In Silesia, for example, the "village church stands without fail in the middle of the cemetery."[3] Similarly, the better-to-do burghers in the provincial towns of Germany were formerly interred in the walls or floor of the church itself. Even if the burial ground is not adjacent to the village church, in which case the word *Friedhof* or *Gottesacker* is used, it still normally enjoys religious sanction. Burial in places other than the sanctified cemetery is uncommon in the rural districts of Central Europe. Within the traditional continental European graveyard, family plots and private ownership of grave sites are virtually un-

FIG. 5-1. the oldest tombstone in the original New Braunfels town cemetery, bearing the date 1851. This beautiful stone, one of the finest to be found in America, displays three *Sechsstern* hex signs. The inscription reads "Hier ruht / Johann Justus Kellner / Geboren d 22t Dezember 1821 / in Braunschweig. / Gestorben den 31t July. 1851 in / Neu Braunfels / Texas. / Friede seiner asche / Friede wohnet hier!" ["Here rests / Johann Justus Kellner / Born December 22, 1821 / in Brunswick. / Died July 31, 1851 in / New Braunfels / Texas / Peace for his ashes / Peace dwells here!"] The base upon which the marker rests bears the inscription of a San Antonio stonecutter, A. Altmann. Photo by the author, 1978.

known, and it has long been the common practice to reuse the site after a few decades have passed.

German burial practices in Texas represent, in site and sanctity, both radical departures from and stubborn loyalty to Central European custom. For some colonists, acculturation advanced rapidly. They accepted very early the southern Anglo-American concept of private, unsanctified family cemeteries. Even in the first half-decade following the founding of New Braunfels and other major colonies, burial of German dead on privately owned farms and ranches began (see box). In Fredericksburg, burials on private town lots occurred as early as 1848, when the settlement was only two years old. In the decades following initial colonization, isolated German family cemeteries became very common in south-central Texas, particularly in the Hill Country (Fig. 5-2).[4] A fine example is the Meusebach-Marschall family graveyard, isolated in a cow pasture near the hamlet of Cherry Spring in Gillespie County. Enclosed by a tall, sturdy rock wall, this burial ground is the last resting place of the Baron von Meusebach, one of the founders of German Texas (Fig. 5-3). The difficulty of transporting dead bodies from remote farms and ranches to the towns no doubt helps to explain the rapid German adoption of the southern family cemetery custom, but often such burial sites were used even when church-related cemeteries were readily available and accessible. Lutheran and Catholic Germans alike buried their dead in unsanctified Texas earth. Most German cemeteries in that state are private family graveyards.

The typically European sanctified, church-related burial ground, or *Kirchhof*, was also established very early by German settlers in Texas and, though less numerous than family cemeteries, the churchly graveyards probably contain more burials than all of the private burial grounds combined (Fig. 5-4). Noteworthy early examples of churchyard cemeteries include Bethlehem Lutheran at Round Top in Fayette County, where interments are made right up to the buttressed walls of the beautiful stone church; St. Martin's Lutheran

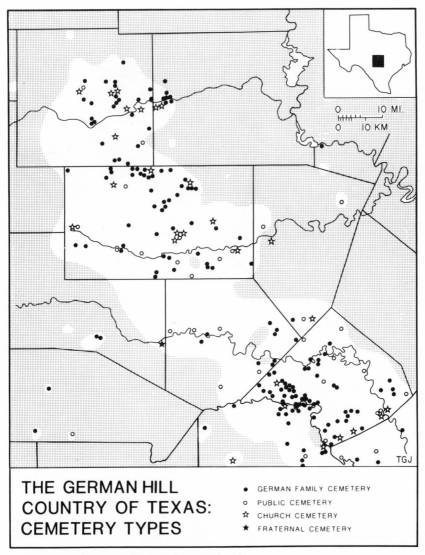

THE GERMAN HILL
COUNTRY OF TEXAS:
CEMETERY TYPES

- ● GERMAN FAMILY CEMETERY
- ○ PUBLIC CEMETERY
- ☆ CHURCH CEMETERY
- ★ FRATERNAL CEMETERY

FIG. 5-2. Note the preponderance of private family cemeteries. The unshaded areas are German populated, centered in the counties of Comal, Kendall, Gillespie, and Mason. Source: field research.

A TEXAS GERMAN FAMILY CEMETERY IS FOUNDED

Some German immigrants abandoned immediately the Central European custom of burial in sanctified church and community cemeteries, adopting the southern custom of private family graveyards. The traveler Ferdinand von Roemer left the following description of a German funeral near New Braunfels in November 1846, barely a year and a half after the founding of the colony: "On November 11th, I attended the funeral of a young girl, the daughter of . . . Mr. K., who had arrived only recently from Germany. . . . Following rural American custom, the people in the funeral procession rode on horseback, a practice that appeared unusual but picturesque to the European eye. Burial was not in the community graveyard, but instead on land belonging to the father of the deceased, as is also the custom in North America. The place of interment selected by the grieving father lay by the beautiful Comal Springs, in sight of same, and shaded by the tall trees of the forest."

—Ferdinand von Roemer,
*Texas: Mit besonderer
Rücksicht auf deutsche
Auswanderung und die
physischen Verhältnisse des
Landes nach eigener
Beobachtung geschildert*, p.
256, translated by the author.

FIG. 5-3. A dry-rock wall surrounds the Meusebach-Marschall family cemetery near Cherry Spring in Gillespie County, almost concealing the tombstone of Baron von Meusebach. The graveyard is located in a pasture, away from the road. Photo by the author, 1975.

in the Hortontown neighborhood of New Braunfels, where a single fence encloses church and graves; and St. Dominic Catholic at Old D'Hanis in Medina County, where the vine-covered, roofless ruin of an Alsatian Gothic church alongside the cemetery lends an Old World and otherworldly flavor to the site (Fig. 5-5). Another German churchyard, at St. John's Evangelical Lutheran in Meyersville in DeWitt County, had been immortalized in a Buck Schiwetz drawing.[5]

Curiously, the establishment of German church-related cemeteries seems to have accelerated after the pioneer period was over, suggesting a "cultural rebound" of Central European traits, paralleling a similar reassertion of Old World culture observed in the agricultural practices of the Germans in Texas.[6] For example, almost forty years passed after initial settlement before, in 1884, rural German Catholics in the community of Comal near New Braunfels petitioned the bishop at

FIG. 5-4. St. Joseph's Catholic Church and cemetery in the rural German community of Honey Creek, Comal County, an example of *Kirchhof* burials. The cemetery was dedicated and sanctified only in 1898; local residents had a long tradition of private family cemeteries prior to that. The smaller wooden crosses on the right mark Mexican graves. Photo by the author, 1975.

FIG. 5-5. The 1893 black-painted iron marker for Pancratius Enderle, against the backdrop of the St. Dominic Catholic Church ruin in Old D'Hanis, Medina County. This cemetery, no longer used, is an excellent example of the typical continental European sanctified churchyard. Photo by the author, 1979.

San Antonio to sanctify a burial site for their hamlet (Fig. 5-6).[7] Lutherans in heavily Germanized Gillespie County acted similarly. In both cases, the establishment of rural, church-related cemeteries was linked to the belated founding of country churches. In German Methodist Mason County, though, the church cemetery at Art was laid out fully four decades after the building of the first chapel.[8]

While probably reflecting a still-remembered Central European tradition of sanctity, these latter-day Texas German churchyards were normally not placed immediately adjacent to the edifice. Rather, they usually lie a hundred yards or more away from the church. At St. Paul Lutheran in Bulverde, Comal County, the cemetery is found across a creek and upstream by several miles from the church, in a different county. Examples of this arrangement can also be found in rural Germany, though the churchyard location is much more common there.

In the German towns of Texas, sanctified community cemeteries were also present from the very first. The sanctity of these graveyards can often be detected only through a search of title deeds. In Fredericksburg, the old city cemetery, designated as the *Kirchhof* on an 1846 map, originally belonged to the town's Protestant union church.[9] When that body splintered into separate Lutheran, Evangelical, Calvinist, and Methodist bodies, the deed remained in the collective ownership of those churches. Only in such freethinker strongholds as Comfort in Kendall County did the German community cemetery lack sanctity. Clearly, the ancient and venerated European custom of burial in sanctified ground survives among the Texas Germans, though some early acculturation occurred. Even the German Methodists, though converted to an Anglo-American southern faith, retain much of the cemetery sanctity sentiment. A German Methodist minister, defrocked for patronizing San Antonio prostitutes, was banished in death to a far corner of a Mason County private family cemetery, where he rests beneath one of the smallest tombstones in the yard.[10]

FIG. 5-6. The sanctity of the German Catholic graveyard at the hamlet of Comal, near New Braunfels, is clearly established by this crucifix. The cemetery dates from 1884, when it was sanctified by the bishop of San Antonio. Photo by the author, 1978.

FIG. 5-7. At the Comfort town cemetery in Kendall County, a German immigrant mother and father lie buried beneath shell-covered cement mounds, probably fashioned in 1921 by craftsman Henry T. Mordhorst of New Braunfels. The shells have been whitewashed. Note that the husband is buried to the left of the wife, differing from southern tradition. Photo by the author, 1979.

Internal Spatial Arrangement

In most respects of internal arrangement, many Texas German cemeteries differ markedly from southern Anglo-American and Mexican graveyards. Such southern traditions as wife-to-the left burial, bordered family plots, and feet-to-east interment are often or generally not adhered to by the Germans (Fig. 5-7). At Meyersville in DeWitt County, for example, the Catholic dead are buried with feet to the south, and in many places the grave axes are aligned with adjacent roads or streets rather than facing the east. In Fredericksburg, both Protestants and Catholics are buried on a northwest-southeast axis, parallel to the main streets of the town. At Muenster in Cooke County, many graves face a central walkway, causing some to be feet-to-west burials. Even the German Methodists occasionally depart from the Wesleyan veneration of feet-to-east interment, as at Bracken in Comal County, where the bordering rural road provides the axis.

Instead of family plots, Texas Germans typically bury only husband and wife side by side. Plots are not privately owned, and the precise place of burial is determined by the annual sequence of deaths. One row of graves might contain the dead of 1917 and 1918, the next row 1919 through 1925, and so on. Separate rows or sections for children are very common, a spatial arrangement unknown among the southern Anglos. As a consequence, each burial is an entity unto itself, a spatial phenomenon clearly revealed by the Texas German custom of providing curbing

for each grave (Fig. 5-8). At Rocky Cemetery in Blanco County, where both Germans and southern Anglo-Americans are buried, the German graves are the only ones to have individual curbing and are easily distinguished visually for that reason. In their use of grave curbing, the Germans closely resemble the Texas Hispanos, but they are perhaps perpetuating a custom still widely seen in Germany today.

Grave curbings sometimes provide an outlet permitting German craftsmen to display their skills at working wood and stone. A re-

FIG. 5-8. The Fredericksburg Catholic Cemetery in Gillespie County displays typically German individual grave curbings and abundant crosses. Graveled walks lie between the graves. Note also the rigid geometric plan of the cemetery, a common German feature. Photo by the author, 1979.

markable assemblage of ornate Teutonic wooden grave curbings can be seen at Frelsburg Lutheran cemetery in Colorado County, though, regrettably, many have deteriorated and been cast aside. Even so, I know of no better surviving collection of decorative wooden curbings in Texas (Fig. 5-9).

Above all, the spatial layout of the Texas German cemetery bespeaks a Teutonic desire for orderliness and symmetry. Let the Anglos, blacks, and Hispanos strew their graves about in a comfortable hodge-podge; the German demands rigid geometry and *Ordnung*.[11]

Tombstones are arranged in neat rows, like soldiers standing rank upon rank, the small stones of children together in one row, the taller monuments of adults in others (Fig. 5-10). If trees are present, they, too, are made to grow as part of a precise geometry. Cedars, placed at regular intervals, adorn some German cemeteries, but randomly spaced native trees will typically be removed. One learns from a Texas German graveyard that there is a proper place for everything, and everything is in its place. Theirs is an orderly universe, in death as in life.

FIG. 5-9. Decaying, deteriorated wooden grave curbing on the Heinsohn family graves in the Lutheran cemetery at Frelsburg in Colorado County. In all likelihood, the curbs were once painted. These are among the very few wooden curbs left in Texas. Photo by the author, 1980.

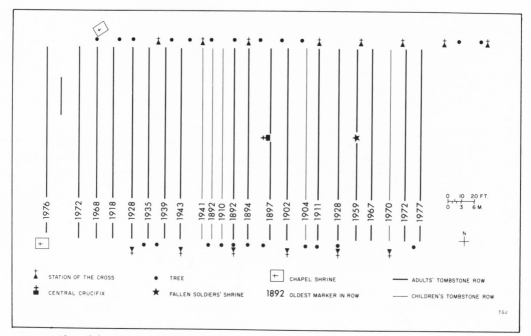

FIG. 5-10. Plan of the St. Peter's Catholic Cemetery, in the churchyard at the German settlement of Lindsay, Cooke County. Note the orderly rows of tombstones, the segregation of children, the treatment of boundaries, and the obvious sanctity. The graves of fallen soldiers are grouped next to their shrine, each equipped with a flag pole. Many trees have died in recent decades, thinning out the once-impressive paling of cedars. Burials are arranged spatially according to the chronological order of death; each row is begun at the south end and progresses northward. Source: field measurements, 1980.

Fences and Perimeters

The enclosing wall or fence, so deeply rooted in the British and southern cemetery traditions, is somewhat less common among the Texas Germans, in spite of abundant Central European prototypes. A great many Teutonic burial grounds in Texas—Catholic, Lutheran, Methodist, and community—lack fences altogether. In this tradition are St. Peter's Roman Catholic at Lindsay in Cooke County, Philadelphia Lutheran at Swiss Alp in Fayette County, and the New Ulm community cemetery in Austin County.

Even so, the graveyard perimeter is often clearly defined. At Lindsay, for example, fourteen sizable stations of the cross, several miniature chapels, and imposing lines of cedar trees mark and guard the border of the cemetery, heightening the orderly, almost military effect conveyed by the neatly aligned rows of tombstones (Fig. 5-10). Similar cedar sentinels guard the perimeter of the German Lutheran churchyard at Quihi in Medina County.

FIG. 5-11. Fence and gate at a German cemetery in Round Top, Fayette County, located in the yard of the Bethlehem Lutheran church. The dry-rock wall is made of slabs of native limestone. Photo by the author, 1979.

Around many other burial grounds, though, the Germans have built enclosing fences, and these often reflect a distinctive Teutonic character. One German family cemetery near Coleto Creek in western Victoria County, now at the bottom of a reservoir, was once enclosed by a picket fence, painted white except for the tips of the pickets, which were a somber black.[12] Even more distinctive are the dry rock fences surrounding scores of German family cemeteries scattered through the pastures of the Texas Hill Country (Fig. 5-3). The compulsion to fence such burial plots was apparently based partly in a desire to keep open-range livestock away from the graves, a need unknown in Germany, where stock were carefully watched by herdsmen. Occasionally, the Texas Germans erected their rock fences around larger, church-related cemeteries, as at St. Mary's Catholic graveyard in Fredericksburg and Bethlehem Lutheran at Round Top in Fayette County (Fig. 5-11). Interestingly,

the Pennsylvania Germans also often enclosed their cemeteries with stone walls, and
the practice can be found in Germany itself.[13]
The sturdy rock fences apparently satisfy a
German desire for permanence.

Even when fenced, the German cemeteries
normally lack the eye-catching lichgates that
adorn most southern graveyards in Texas. In
the few cases where German lichgates do occur, they exist mainly to reinforce the sanctity of the cemetery rather than merely to
announce the name and to designate the
proper entryway (Fig. 5-12). At Cave Creek
Lutheran in Gillespie County, the metal arch
of the lichgate is topped with a cross and
bears the inscription "I am the Resurrection
and the Life"—features unthinkable in a traditional southern cemetery.

FIG. 5-12. An ornate lichgate at the German cemetery in Walburg, Williamson County. Somewhat unusual among the Texas Germans, lichgates, when
present, reinforce the sanctity of graveyards
through use of the cross symbol and denomina-
tional names. Photo by the author, 1981.

Landscaping and Grave Decoration

Many Texas German cemeteries are grass
covered, and the frequent mowings required
in summer are facilitated by the neat rowing
of tombstones. Frequently, though, "scraping"
is practiced, particularly when individual
grave curbings are present (Figs. 2-2, 5-8). The
narrow walkways between the curbings are
often graveled rather than grassy, a feature
also seen in the ancestral home villages of the
Texas Germans in Central Europe. Most
likely, though, Texas German graveyard scraping was adopted from the local southerners as
an expedient way to cope with the problem of
rapid grass growth in a subtropical climate.

Also apparently representing acculturation
is the widespread Texas German use of shell
decoration on graves (Fig. 2-10). I have never
seen such decoration in the European villages
that sent settlers to Texas, though, reportedly,
shells appeared on graves in some parts of
northern Germany as recently as the nineteenth century.[14] But even if the Germans
adopted shell decoration from the Anglos or
Hispanos, they unquestionably lent it their
own distinctive character. In New Braunfels,
for example, an unusual funerary artform developed. Using marine bivalve shells carefully
selected for unflawed appearance and unifor-
mity of size and shape, a local German craftsman fashioned graceful, round-topped grave
mounds (see box). He pressed shells into wet
concrete, forming perfect, straight rows that
produced a visually striking effect (Fig. 5-7).
The entire mound often acquired a coat of
white or black paint, heightening the emotional impact of the shell-covered mound.
The work of this craftsman, and possibly of
some imitators, diffused from New Braunfels
widely through Comal and all neighboring
counties in the early twentieth century. Un-
fortunately, hailstorms, frost, and vandals
have taken a heavy toll of these cement shell
mounds, and completely undamaged specimens are increasingly difficult to find.

Certain other grave decorations are even
more distinctively German or continental European. Particularly in Catholic cemeteries,
metal wreath boxes with glass lids are often

propped against tombstones, within the curbing (Fig. 5-13). German Catholic candle holders, covered as shelter from the weather, stand atop graves in some cemeteries.

The Texas Germans have adopted many traditional southern graveyard plants, such as the crape myrtle and iris. Cedars or other evergreens are almost invariably present, perpetuating an ancient pagan custom that is as much Teutonic as British-southern. Curiously, the use of the pomegranate as a cemetery plant in Texas seems to be most common among the Germans. One might expect this many-seeded fertility symbol, linked to the great Mediterranean mother goddess and the Madonna, to occur most commonly in southern or Hispanic, rather than German, graveyards, but its principal concentration seems to lie in Comal, Gillespie, Mason, and Llano counties—the heart of the German-settled Hill Country.[15]

Grave Markers

The Texas Germans, in common with southerners and Mexicans, fashion grave markers from several different materials, particularly wood, metal, and stone. Each has European German antecedents. It is fair to say, I believe, that the craftsmanship displayed by these German markers is more highly developed than that of the Anglos, blacks, and Hispanos (Fig. 5-14).[16] The quality of work is consistently high and occasionally superb, perhaps because the German population in Texas included more persons skilled in working wood, metal, and stone than did the other groups. Possibly, too, the Germans placed a higher value on ornate, well-crafted memorials to the dead or their notion of ornateness differed from those of the southerners and Mexicans. Whatever the reason, German cemeteries in Texas offer the visitor some remarkable visual delights. Similarities between German grave markers in Texas, Pennsylvania, and Central Europe suggest that the forms and skills evident in Texas reflect an imported tradition rather than one which developed locally.

"MADE BY H. T. MORDHORST, NEW BRAUNFELS, TEX."

The inscription above was found on a well-crafted, shell-decorated concrete grave cover. Sara Clark tells us more about this Mecklenburger craftsman:

"Henry Theodore Mordhorst was a cement finisher who lived in New Braunfels from 1900 until his death in 1928. He was born in 1864 in Rostock, Germany, and came to the United States in 1882 with his mother and three sisters after the death of his father. . . . In making his grave covers, Mordhorst first made a flat concrete base on which a wooden form was placed to mold the concrete. He used wire mesh . . . to give the concrete support internally when it was poured into the mold. The shells were filled with cement, and a wire was twisted into each one to help hold the shell to the grave cover. He arrived at this method of attaching the shells by experimentation after his earlier shells came off too easily. He ordered the cockleshells from Rockport and Galveston; they arrived by train in big barrels. . . . No one knows where Henry Mordhorst first got the idea for the beautiful shell-decorated grave covers that he made. They do not seem to be modeled closely after anything he knew in Germany."

—Sara Clark, "The Decoration of Graves in Central Texas with Seashells," in *Diamond Bessie and the Shepherds*, Publications of the Texas Folklore Society, No. 36, pp. 37–38; ©Texas Folklore Society, reprinted with permission.

FIG. 5-13. A glassed wreath box wired to the Frank Zeiner tombstone in the Catholic cemetery at Frelsburg in Colorado County. Such decoration appears to be distinctively Central European Catholic. The Zeiner epitaph lists his birthplace as the village of Böhm.[isch] Rothwasser in the year 1846. This village now lies in Czechoslovakia but had a German-speaking population until 1945. Photo by the author, 1980.

FIG. 5-14. German metalwork craftsmanship displayed in an isolated rural cemetery in the Texas Hill Country. This dignified memorial to Meda Emma Klar, a five-month-old child, stands in the Catholic cemetery at Honey Creek in Comal County. The marker is painted silver, with black lettering, and the epitaph translates as "The innocent on earth / are assured of Heaven." Photo by the author, 1978.

Most often when German craftsmen worked in wood to produce grave markers, they fashioned crosses of one type or another. Indeed, the cross is one of the most commonly used symbols in Texas German cemeteries, among Catholics and Lutherans alike. Rather than producing simple Latin crosses like those of the Hispanos, though, the German woodworkers often turned out elaborate and unusual variations (Fig. 5-15). Some are nicely fluted, while others have designs cut by jigsaw. The most impressive collection of wooden crosses that I have seen in Texas stands in St. Mary's churchyard, the center of a German Catholic ethnic island north of Plantersville in Grimes County (Fig. 5-16).

FIG. 5-15. A deteriorating but still dignified wooden cross, lobed at the points and carefully bolted together, stands in the St. Mary's Catholic cemetery near Plantersville in Grimes County. Texas Germans frequently fashioned ornate wooden crosses for grave markers. Photo by the author, 1980.

FIG. 5-16. A distinctive fluted wooden cross in the German Catholic St. Mary's cemetery near Plantersville, Grimes County. The marker appears to be of recent manufacture and perhaps replaced an older marker of similar design. Photo by the author, 1980.

FIG. 5-17. Joseph Rudinger, an Alsatian, carved the hauntingly beautiful Catharina Garteiser tombstone in 1861, and it still stands in the St. Dominic German Catholic churchyard at Old D'Hanis, Medina County. The figure perhaps represents God standing atop the Earth. An epitaph, a decorative "turnip" heart, and the carver's inscription "BY JOSEPH RUDIᴎGER 1861" appear on the reverse side. Photo by the author, 1979.

Wooden forms other than the cross are less common among the Texas Germans, but some boards with jigsaw-cut tops are seen here and there (Fig. 6-4).[17]

German stonecutters, working mainly with soft white Texas limestone, equaled and surpassed the woodworkers in producing impressive grave markers. Some of their most striking monuments are antebellum in origin and appear to be clustered in the Hill Country and the Alsatian communities of Medina County. The 1851 Johann Justus Kellner tombstone in the old community cemetery at New Braunfels is one of the finest folk tombstones that I have seen in the United States (Fig. 5-1). Though much damaged, the Kellner stone, weathered to shades of amber and brown, remains lovely and is distinguished by the ornate use of Gothic arches, flowers, and stars. Equally impressive is a stone in the St. Dominic Catholic cemetery in Old D'Hanis, Medina County (Fig. 5-17). Carved about 1861 by Joseph Rudinger, an immigrant from Alsace, this stone features a haunting hooded and robed figure standing atop a small globe. Scrolls adorn the lower part of the limestone monument, and Rudinger carefully carved his name, along with an epitaph, on the opposite side. Even after the advent of precut, exotic stone, local German craftsmen continued to produce beautifully fashioned inscriptions in the German Gothic script (Fig. 1-1).[18]

It is in metalwork that German grave marker craftsmanship finds its most distinctive expression. The range is from relatively simple strip metal with attached decoration to highly ornate decorative wrought or molded ironwork. Representative of the simple style is the 1907 Katharina Simon monument, hidden away in a rural Catholic graveyard in Comal County (Fig. 5-18). Decorating the silver-painted Latin Cross are scrolls, eight-petaled flowers, and a dignified porcelain epitaph disc. Also in the simple style is a curious undated metal monument, possibly intended to be a stylistic human figure, in a Grimes County German cemetery (Fig. 5-19) and a cross topped with a graceful arch in Old D'Hanis (Fig. 5-20). The 1894 Anna Syring marker from rural Comal County appears to

FIG. 5-18. This simple sheet metal cross, painted silver and adorned with stylistic flowers or sun wheels, is in the Honey Creek Catholic cemetery near Anhalt in western Comal County. The epitaph, on a porcelain disk, reads "Hier ruht / Katharina Simon / geb. zu Mitzai Elsass / den 12. Okt. 1818 / gest. zu Anhalt den 1. marz 1907" ["Here rests / Katharina Simon / born at Mitzai, Alsace / October 12, 1818 / died at Anhalt March 1, 1907"]. Photo by the author, 1978.

FIG. 5-19. A strikingly distinctive, yet simple metal grave marker in St. Mary's German churchyard near Plantersville, Grimes County. The marker may be a stylistic human figure, but the top arc is the ancient Germanic *Urbogen*, describing the path of the sun through the sky at the winter solstice. Photo by the author, 1980.

FIG. 5-20. A metal cross with a graceful canopy bar, marking the 1887 Johanna Garteiser burial at the St. Dominic churchyard in Old D'Hanis, Medina County. Virtually identical canopy bars exist in Central Europe. Schwindrazheim, in his book *Deutsche Bauernkunst*, p. 234, shows an example from Hessen-Nassau. Photo by the author, 1979.

FIG. 5-21. The silver-painted Anna Syring metal
grave marker at Comal Catholic cemetery near
New Braunfels is noteworthy for its hex signs and
related symbolism, including three Teutonic hearts
at the apexes of the cross, the pentacle *Drudenfuss*
near the base, and the quartered sunbursts where
the two bars join. Most likely, this marker was cast
by the Alamo Iron Works in San Antonio. Photo by
the author, 1978.

Hier ruht in Christo!
Wilhelm Herbort
geb. den 3. Dec. 1854.
gest. den 7. Juni 1917.

have been made of molded iron (Fig. 5-21). Most such cast iron markers, in south-central parts of the state at least, were produced by the Alamo Iron Works in San Antonio.

In a class by themselves are some highly intricate decorative ironwork markers, apparently produced by local craftsmen. The Meda Emma Klar monument in Comal County is a typical example and dates from 1901 (Fig. 5-14). Most exquisite of all are the Emma and Wilhelm Herbort wrought iron markers, side by side in the Cave Creek Lutheran cemetery near Fredericksburg (Figs. 5-22, 5-23). These truly exceptional, beautifully crafted metal monuments represent an old tradition rooted in Central Europe and only rarely encountered in America.[19] Also impressive are decorative metal wreaths, intended for placement in boxes at the base of tombstones, but very few of these have survived the ravages of weather and antique thieves (Fig. 5-24).

FIG. 5-23. The Emma Herbort marker, also at Cave Creek, provides an exquisite companion for the adjacent one shown in Fig. 5-22, while still displaying its own special character. Photo by the author, 1977.

FIG. 5-24. A rusted metal wreath stands exposed to the weather on a 1924 grave in Frelsburg Lutheran Cemetery, Colorado County. The glass lid that once protected it has broken. Photo by the author, 1980.

FIG. 5-22 (*opposite*). Perhaps the finest example of German metal funerary craftsmanship is the 1917 Wilhelm Herbort marker in the St. Paul Lutheran Cemetery at rural Cave Creek in Gillespie County. Similar markers occur in Hessen-Nassau, one of the main sources of Gillespie County Germans; see Schwindrazheim, *Deutsche Bauernkunst*, p. 234. Photo by the author, 1977.

Hex Signs and Related Symbols

The Texas Germans traditionally adorned
grave markers with one or, more typically,
multiple hex symbols, all of which are trace-
able to the Old World. Some are linked directly to medieval and pre-Christian witch-
craft, but they may have lost some or all of
their original pagan meaning by the time of
the Texas migration. Even if they no longer
bore their ancient messages, these signs at
least lent still more distinctiveness to the
Texas German graveyard. Often, the hex signs
appear in multiples of two, three, or even four
or five on an individual stone, producing a
pagan visual effect (Figs. 5-25, 5-30).

One of the most common traditional symbols is the venerable Teutonic *Sonnenrad*, or
"sun wheel," derived from a pre-Christian sun
cult among the Germanic tribes. Several varieties of sun wheels appear on Texas German
grave markers. Perhaps most jolting to the
non-Teutonic eye is the ancient Aryan swastika, or *Hakenkreuz*, a happy symbol of the
sun long before its meaning was forever
changed and corrupted by the Nazis (Fig.
5-26). In Texas, as in Pennsylvania and North
Carolina, the funerary swastika normally appears in the less sinister "whirling" form.
Some notable examples occur on both Catholic and Protestant tombstones in Fredericksburg, dating from the period prior to about
1880. However, the swastika is rare in Texas,
and other sun symbols enjoyed preference,
as is also true among the Pennsylvania
Germans.[20]

Much more common Texas German sun
wheels are six- and eight-pointed figures. Perhaps most pleasing to the eye is the six-
pointed compass star, a type of *Sechsstern* in
which the points take on a rounded configuration to resemble a stylistic petaled flower
(Figs. 5-1, 5-27, 5-30). In this form, the
Sechsstern also appears frequently on tombstones in Pennsylvania German graveyards, as
well as in Lower Saxony and other parts of
Germany that contributed to the Texas migration.[21] Other *Sonnenrad* hex signs found in
Texas and Germany have straight lines representing the sun's rays and resemble asterisks

FIG. 5-25. The Christian cross competes for space
and importance with five medieval hex signs on the
1873 L[orenz] Steinmetz tombstone in the old town
cemetery at New Braunfels. Three of the signs are
eight-pointed "asterisk" sun symbols and the other
two are six-pointed stars, or *Sechssterne*. Steinmetz
was a Hessian born in 1802 in the vineyard village
of Oestrich, Nassau, on the Rhine River. Photo by
the author, 1978.

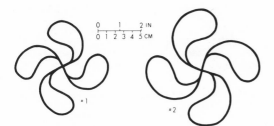

FIG. 5-26. Whirling swastikas on two German tombstones in Gillespie County in the Texas Hill Country. Key: #1, Emiela Roder stone, 1880, Fredericksburg Catholic cemetery; #2, Dobette Henke stone, 1876, Fredericksburg Protestant cemetery. In each case, the swastika appeared twice on the stone. Also, both of the deceased died in infancy. Redrawn from rubbings made in 1979 by the author.

FIG. 5-27. Selected six-pointed hex signs derived from rubbings of Texas German gravestones: 1, compass *Sechsstern*, Fredericksburg Protestant cemetery, Gillespie County, 1878, Amalie Arhelger stone (family from Hessen); 2, hexagram *Drudenfuss*, Castroville cemetery, Medina County, 1867, Biry stone (family from Alsace); 3, hexagram *Drudenfuss*, Salem Lutheran cemetery, Rose Hill, Harris County, 1876, Franciska Voebel stone; 4, double *Sechsstern Drudenfuss*, New Braunfels old town cemetery, Comal County, 1874, E. A. Gottfried Vogt stone; 5, *Sechsstern Drudenfuss*, Fredericksburg Protestant cemetery, Gillespie County, 1870, Johann Durst stone (family from Württemberg); 6, compass *Sechsstern* sun wheel, St. Mary's Catholic churchyard, near Plantersville, Grimes County, 1935, G. M. Winkler stone; 7, compass *Sechsstern* sun wheel, Fredericksburg Protestant cemetery, Gillespie County, undated, anonymous stone; 8, *Sechsstern* sun wheel, New Braunfels old town cemetery, Comal County, 1873, appears twice on stone, L[orenz] Steinmetz stone (family from Hessen). The asymmetries are accurately drawn.

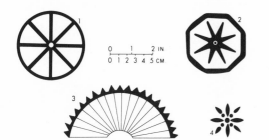

FIG. 5-28. Selected sun symbols, derived from rubbings of Texas German gravestones: 1, "wagon-wheel" type sun wheel, Comfort cemetery, Kendall County, 1921, Marie Strube stone; 2, "asterisk" sun wheel, New Braunfels old town cemetery, Comal County, 1873, stone of L[orenz] Steinmetz (born in Hessen), symbol appears three times on stone; 3, half sunburst, New Braunfels old town cemetery, Comal County, 1869, stone of Johan Jost Nickel (born in Hessen); 4, eight-lobed compass sun wheel, Fischer Cemetery, Comal County, 1874, stone of Heinrich Coers (born in Lower Saxony). The asymmetries are accurately shown.

or wagon wheels (Fig. 5-28).[22] Occasionally, half- or quarter-sunbursts appear on German Texan markers, apparently also duplicating an Old World and Pennsylvania custom (Figs. 5-21, 5-28).[23]

A related symbol is the pagan *Urbogen*, a gentle arc believed to signify the low path of the sun through the sky at the winter solstice (Fig. 6-1). In German folk art, the *Urbogen* connotes good luck, and it somewhat resembles a horseshoe. The ends of the arc must point downward, however, since they represent sunrise and sunset.[24] The *Urbogen* is rare in Texas, and even when such arcs occur, the observer cannot always be certain that the ancient solstice symbolism is intended (Fig. 5-19).

The *Drudenfuss*, or "witch's foot," hex sign, believed to ward off evil spirits and the Devil, appears as a five- and six-pointed star (Fig. 5-27). Among the Pennsylvania Germans, the term *hexefiess*, also meaning "witch's foot," is preferred.[25] The six-pointed variety, or hexagram, is also, along with the previously mentioned compass star, called a *Sechsstern* (Fig. 5-27). The equally common pentacle, or five-pointed *Drudenfuss*, is sometimes called a *Pentagramm* (Fig. 5-29).[26] It can easily be mistaken in Texas German folk art for the lone star symbol of the state, but it is no such thing (Figs. 5-21, 6-1).

The significance of the *Drudenfuss* in general, and the pentacle in particular, to the medieval German is suggested by a scene from Goethe's *Faust*. On the threshold of the door leading into Faust's study was a pentacle. One of its points, facing the outside, was poorly drawn, with the tip of the point left a bit open. Mephistopheles, because of this imperfection, was able to enter Faust's study, but in order to leave, he had to command a rat to gnaw away one of the correctly formed, inward-pointing apexes.[27] In Texas, I have seen many pentacles on tombstones, but never one with a flawed point.

In addition to the *Sonnenrad, Urbogen*, and *Drudenfuss*, Germans make frequent use of the heart motif in their funerary folk art (see box; Figs. 5-30, 5-31).[28] A traditional Teutonic symbol of love and life, the heart helps lend

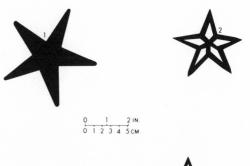

FIG. 5-29. The pentacle *Drudenfuss*, derived from rubbings of selected Texas German tombstones: 1, Frelsburg Catholic cemetery, Colorado County, undated, native stone; 2, Boerne Cemetery, Kendall County, 1873, Caroline Steinheil stone; 3, St. Paulus Lutheran Cemetery, Bexar County, bas relief, 1909, Emil Rieger footstone; 4, Comal cemetery, New Braunfels, Comal County, 1897, Benedikt Kaderli stone (born 1852 in Mülch, Canton Bern, Switzerland). The asymmetries are accurately drawn. In medieval Germanic folklore, the pentacle was believed to ward off the Devil.

FIG. 5-30. At Castroville, Medina County, the 1864
tombstone of Benjamin Biry, an Alsatian, is adorned
with two nicely cut six-pointed compass sun
wheels, or *Sechssterne*, and two Teutonic concave-
pointed hearts, one of which is crossed by anchor
and sword to form the Catholic *mater dolorosa*.
The stone has fallen and now lies in the cemetery
grass. Photo by the author, 1979.

THE GERMAN HEART

"In the course of time the heart was accepted as
the seat of the human emotions and took its
place in German peasant art as the favored
symbol of love. In its earlier connotations it
symbolized the all-bearing Mother Earth,
sometimes in conjunction with the swastika
and the six-point compass star as symbols of the
sun, under whose rays the earth will once more
bear fruits. Now and then it signified motherhood in general. As the token of love and human
affections it is found everywhere in folk art and
continued to be a most favored symbol among
our German pioneers in Pennsylvania, whether
in a secular sense . . . or with a religious
significance . . . on tombstones."

—Preston A. Barba,
*Pennsylvania German
Tombstones*, Volume 18 of
the Pennsylvania German
Folklore Society, 1953, p. 24;
© Pennsylvania German
Folklore Society, 1954,
reprinted with permission.

FIG. 5-31. The Teutonic "turnip-shaped" heart in bas relief adorns the Theresie Zurcher monument in the St. Dominic churchyard, Old D'Hanis, Medina County. Inside the heart are flowers, possibly intended to represent the Germanic "tree of life" motif that is so common in Germany and among the Pennsylvania "Dutch." Photo by the author, 1979.

the German graveyard a special character, even though, as mentioned in Chapters 3 and 4, the heart also appears occasionally in southern and Hispanic tombstone art (Fig. 3-24). Typically, the distinctive Teutonic turnip-shaped heart, with a concave point, is employed, sometimes crossed by the anchor and sword to form the *mater dolorosa* (Fig. 5-30).[29] Others appear in conjunction with sun wheels, witch's feet, or the cross, fashioned in wood, stone, and metal alike (Figs. 5-32, 5-33, 5-34).

Interestingly, the swastika, six-pointed compass star, and heart all appear abundantly in Basque folk art, suggesting that they may

FIG. 5-32. The undated metal grave marker of John Speies in the Fredericksburg Catholic cemetery features a cross attached atop a heart and flanked by two protective hexagram witch's feet. Photo by the author, 1979.

be truly ancient European symbols. Their occurrence in Texas is, at the very least, a perpetuation of a Germanic custom with long-forgotten roots in pagan times. The conservatism of the folk graveyard is again evident.

Another typical German tombstone decoration, apparently of more recent origin, is a picture of the deceased. The earliest versions, dating from the latter part of the nineteenth century, are oil paintings protected by a glass window. More durable are photographs transferred to porcelain, a type that became very common around the turn of the century (Fig. 5-35). The portraits add a very personal touch to the German monuments.

FIG. 5-34. The top bar of a 1910 German Catholic wooden grave marker, commemorating a member of the Friesenhahn family in St. Joseph's near Comal, Comal County, displays a jigsaw-cut inverted Teutonic heart and confrontal symbols possibly intended to be crescent and full moons, a common tombstone decoration in Germany. Photo by the author, 1978.

FIG. 5-33. In Castroville, Medina County, the heart provides a place for the epitaph on the 1881 metal cross commemorating Alsatian André Briden, born, according to the faded inscription, in the village of Oberentzen, near Colmar in the Rhine plain, in the year 1808. Photo by the author, 1979.

German Language Epitaphs

In Germany, the use of epitaphs dates to at least the middle of the sixteenth century, and the practice still flourishes there.[30] Texas offers some notable examples for the period 1850 to 1940, including some in the folk tradition.

The German language found abundant written expression in Texas, in newspapers, almanacs, and even literature. None of these printed formats is likely to prove as durable as the epitaphs engraved in native Texas stone—a medium of such permanence as to allow the German language to survive in the graveyards long after the spoken tongue is dead.[31] Too, the epitaph allows us to look deeply into the Texas German soul, to probe the immigrants' innermost feelings about life, the abandoned fatherland, and death.

FIG. 5-35. A porcelain portrait of a young man adorns his tombstone in the Catholic cemetery at Westphalia in Falls County. Photo by the author, 1980.

I have transcribed the epitaphs presented below exactly as they were, including errors and archaic spellings, and have translated them literally, rather than attempting to retain meter and rhyme. As a rule, Texas German epitaphs are longer, more poetic, and more informative than those of the southerners and Hispanos. Maiden names are normally given, and the reader can also learn much about the specific currents of migration that brought Germans to the Texas shores. Many Central European provinces and even villages of birth are listed (Figs. 1-1, 5-1, 5-13, 5-18). Such information might best be regarded as symptomatic of a profound homesickness never cured, a resistance to being buried in the Texas earth without a parting cry admonishing the passerby: "Do not forget that I was a German, that these alien plains and hills are no proper resting place for me." The epitaph of Johann Lamon in Castroville beautifully expresses this homesickness and also caters to the German love of rhymes:

> Ich starb hier im fremden Land
> Doch ich ruh' in Gotteshand
> Wie in meinem lieben Vaterland
> [I died here in a foreign land
> Still I rest in God's hands
> Just like in my beloved fatherland]
>   (1882, Castroville, Medina
>   County)

We see it, too, in the heartfelt Teutonic outcry, the spelling already flawed by English influence, in a North Texas prairie graveyard:

> Hier ruht die tugendreiche Yungfrau
> und Farmerstochter Rosina Maier
> Geb. am 25 Feb. 1882 in
> Auggenbach in Bayern, Deutschland
> [Here rests the virtuous young woman
> and farmer's daughter Rosina Maier
> Born on Feb. 25, 1882, in
> Auggenbach in Bavaria, Germany]
>   (Pilot Point St. Thomas
>   Catholic, Denton County)

German epitaphs, like those of the southern Anglo-American and black, fall into a number of distinct categories. None is richer or more poignant than the tradition of the "speaking dead," in which the deceased are made to pass on words of comfort or wisdom to the survivors. One of the best of this type, on the Joseph Zurcher stone, is also among the oldest surviving German inscriptions in Texas. It has suffered damage and will soon become illegible as the soft limestone weathers away. Beneath a protective pentacle *Drudenfuss* we read, in relentless rhymes:

> Horch' was der todte Vater spricht.
> Ihr hinterlassene weinet nicht.
> Seid treu dem Glauben u.[nd] Pflicht.
> Tragt euer K.[reuz] der Leidensch.[aft]
>   Genicht.[32]
> Und tretet, wenn das Herz einbricht.
> Mit Freuden vor des Hern Gericht

[Hear what the dead father says.
You who are left behind, do not cry.
Be loyal to your faith a.[nd] duty.
Bear your c.[ross] of suffer.[ing] gladly.
And when your hearts break, step.
With joy before the Lord's judgement.]
(1860, St. Dominic Catholic
Cemetery, Old D'Hanis,
Medina County)

Another very old Catholic inscription in the speaking-dead tradition, similarly flawed in spelling, is found in the eastern part of the Texas German belt:

O lieber Freund gedenke mein
In dein Gebet mich schlüsse[33] ein
Lebe stets als frommer Christ,
Der seine Pflichten nicht vergist.
Bereite dich zu jeder zeit
Und sorge für die Ewigkeit
[O dear friend remember me
Include me in your prayer
Live always as a pious Christian,
Who does not forget his duties
Prepare yourself at all times
And be concerned for eternity.]
(1856, Frelsburg Catholic
Cemetery, Colorado County

Protestants also wrote epitaphs in the speaking-dead tradition. One of the most memorable begins by giving a clue, in German already corrupted by English, about a murderer's identity:

Ermordet bei
Bekannter Hand
J.M. M.G. G.W.
Bin ich todt? O nein, ihr
Lieben. Oben strömt
das Leben frei. Aller
Todt ist drunten blieben,
Alles Starben ist vorbei!
Wollt ihr wissen wie es
geht? Kommet höher,
Kommt und seht.
[Murdered by
the hand of someone I knew
J.M. M.G. G.W.
Am I dead? Oh no, you

dear ones. Here above life
goes on. All
Death remained there below,
All dying is over!
Would you like to know how it
is? Come up higher, Come and see]
(Quihi, Medina County)

Others are less violent and more biblical in nature:

Ich bin ein Gast auf Erden
Und hab hier keinen Stand,
Der Himmel soll mir werden
Da ist mein Vaterland
[I am a guest on earth
And have no standing here
Heaven shall be mine
There is my Fatherland]
(1902, Methodist, Rose Hill
Cemetery, Harris County)

Lebt wohl, ihr Lieben,
Klagt nicht mehr,
Ich musst euch lassen einsam
hier, sanft schlumre ich im Schattenland
Bis uns vereint ein ewig Land
[Farewell, dear ones,
complain no more,
I had to leave you alone
here, softly I slumber in shadowland
Until an eternal Land unites us.]
(date illegible, New
Braunfels original town
cemetery, Comal County)

The epitaphs of children and young adults also often reflect the speaking-dead tradition:

Ich war der Mutter Trost
Dem Vater eine Freude,
Gott aber liebt' mich mehr
Denn diese alle beide
Kaum blüht ich auf
Da fiel ich ab
Fiel aus der Wiege
In das Grab
[I was my mother's comfort
A pleasure to my father,
But God loved me more
Than do these two
Hardly had I blossomed

Before I fell off
Fell from the cradle
Into the grave.]

(1884, 2-year-old child, New
Braunfels original town
cemetery, Comal County)

In meiner Jugend Lebensziel
Rief mich der Herr zur Ewigkeit
Vater und Mutter tröstet euch
Ich bin jetzt in Himmelreich
[At the end of my youth
The Lord called me to eternity
Father and mother be comforted
I am now in the Kingdom of Heaven]

(1878, 23-year-old woman,
Methodist, Lower Willow
Cemetery, Mason County)

Equally moving, and also usually rhymed, are
epitaphs in the "speaking to the dead" style:

So schlummre sanft, Du guter Vater
Das Grab entriss Dich uns zu früh
Du warst uns Schutz. Du warst
    Berather[34]
Ach, wir vergessen Deiner nie.
[So slumber gently, you good father,
The grave tore you from us too early
You were our protector. You were our
    counselor
Oh, we will never forget you.]

(1896, New Braunfels
original town cemetery,
Comal County)

Ruhe sanft
in kühlen
Grunde
Bis zur auf-
erstehungs
Stunde
[Rest gently
in the cool
ground
Until the Re-
surrection's
hour]

(1908, Lutheran, Frelsburg,
Colorado County)

Traurig blicken wir dir nach
In dein stilles Schlafgemach
Glauben an ein Auferstehn
Freuen uns auf's Wiedersehn
[Sadly we gaze after you
In your quiet place of sleep
We believe in the Resurrection
And look forward to seeing you again.]

(1884, Peter and Paul
Catholic Cemetery,
Meyersville, DeWitt County)

Guter Onkel
unsere Thränen
Sind wie Blumen
auf dem Grab
[Good uncle
our tears
are like flowers
on the grave.]

(1897, Hilda Methodist
Cemetery, Mason County)

Ach hier nicht mehr, ach fern
von mir bist Du. Ich seh' nichts
mehr von Dir. Du liebe arme
Seele. Entflohn aus meinen
Armen, weit aus diesem Thal
der sterblichkeit bist Du
liebste Seele
[Oh, here no more, oh, far away
from me are you. I see no
more of you. You poor dear
soul. You have fled from my
arms, far away from this valley
of mortality,
dear soul]

(1879, Salem Lutheran
Cemetery, Rose Hill, Harris
County)

Schlaf süsz in kalter Erde
Nichts störe deine Ruh
Und Rasen grün und duftend
Deck deine Asche zu
[Sleep sweetly in the cold earth
May nothing disturb your rest
And may a green and fragrant lawn
Cover your ashes]

(probably a Freethinker,
Twin Sisters Cemetery,
Blanco County)

Endlich hast Du überwunden
Manche schwere, harte Stunden
Manchen Tag und manche Nacht
Hast Du in Schmerzen zugebracht
Standhaft hast Du sie ertragen
Deine Schmerzen, deine Plagen,
Bis der Tod Dein Auge brach.
Doch Du bist im Himmel wach
[Finally you have overcome
Many difficult, hard hours
Many days and many nights
You have spent in pain
Steadfastly you endured them
Your pains, your miseries,
Until death dimmed your eyes
But you are awake in Heaven]
                    (1908, Fredericksburg
                    Catholic Cemetery,
                    Gillespie County)

O wier sehens uns in bessern Welten
Denn zu gut warst Du fur diese hier,
Wo der Himmelsvater wird vergelten
Mutterlieb und Gattentreue dir
[Oh, we will see each other in better
    worlds
For you were too good for this one here,
Where the Heavenly Father will reward
    you
For mother's love and faithfulness to
    spouse]
                    (New Braunfels original
                    town cemetery, Comal
                    County)

Other epitaphs are directed at passersby,
eulogizing the deceased or telling something
about their death:

Clärchen war ein liebes
gutes Kind
Fromm wie die Engel
sind
[Little Clara was a dear
good child
Pious like the angels
are]
                    (1914, 2-year-old child,
                    Germania Lutheran
                    Cemetery, Lee County)

Was die Mutter uns gewesen.
Kann man nicht am Grabstein lesen.
Eingegraben wie in Erz.
Ist es in der Kinder Herz.
Gott der Herr der Welten. soll's ihr
Tausendfach vergelten.
[What our mother was to us.
You cannot read on the tombstone.
Engraved as if in bronze.
Is it in the hearts of the children.
God the Lord of the worlds. Shall
Reward her a thousandfold.]
                    (1941, Catholic cemetery,
                    Westphalia, Falls County)

Sein Leben war
ein Augenblick
Ein Frühlingstraum
sein Erdenglück
[His life was
but an instant
A springtime dream
was his earthly fortune]
                    (1894, infant, cemetery near
                    Round Top, Fayette County)

Thränen fliesset, rinnet
Wohl um den Edlen hier!
Blumen spriesset, blühet
Zu des Todten Ehr
[Let tears flow, run
For our noble friend here!
Let flowers bloom and grow
In honor of this dead one!]
                    (1879, probably Freethinker,
                    Boerne Cemetery, Kendall
                    County)

Some of these were apparently taken from
German-language stonecutters' verse books,
which were widely used in America. Others
are clearly original, as is revealed by their
unique content and grammatical errors. Two
epitaphs in a rural Catholic graveyard in the
Hill Country are wonderful examples of locally composed verses:

Es war ein unschuldig's Kindlein
dieses Friedhof's Grundstein
[It was an innocent little child
Whose burial founded this cemetery]
                    (1899)

Des Morgens Schlangen Biss macht
Abends Dir den Himmel g'wiss
[A snake bite in the morning makes
Heaven certain for you by evening]
>
> (1901, children, Honey
> Creek St. Joseph's Catholic
> Cemetery, Anhalt, Comal
> County)

Another one-of-a-kind epitaph comes from the Houston area. Mr. H. W. Hoffman, it informs us,

> . . . starb einen
> ehrenvollen Tod in
> der Ausübung sei-
> ner Amtspflicht als
> Deputy Sheriff in
> Fulshear, Fort Bend
> Co., Texas
> [. . . died an
> honorable death in
> the performance of his
> official duty as
> Deputy Sheriff in
> Fulshear, Fort Bend
> Co., Texas]
>
> > (1893, Salem Lutheran
> > Cemetery, Rose Hill, Harris
> > County)

Unionists executed by Confederate officials following a skirmish in the Hill Country were:

> Gefangen genommen
> und ermordet
> [Taken captive
> and murdered]
>
> > (ca. 1865, one face of the
> > monument to the Unionist
> > dead, Comfort, Kendall
> > County)

Other epitaphs pass on peasant wisdom and piety:

> Die gerechten Seelen
> Sind in Gottes Hand
> In des Friedens ew'gen
> Faterland[35]

[The righteous souls
are in God's hand
In the eternal
Fatherland of peace]
>
> (1917, Rocky Cemetery,
> Blanco County)

Gatten aus dem arm des Gatten
Eltern aus der Kinder Creis
Dekt des Todes stiller Schatten
Er umfängt Kind, Jüngling, Greis
[Spouse taken out of the arms of spouse
Parents taken out of the company of their
children
Covered by death's still shadow
Which embraces child, youth, and the
aged alike]
>
> (1869, St. Dominic Catholic
> Cemetery, Old D'Hanis,
> Medina County)

Trachtet nach dem
das droben ist
und nicht nach dem
was auf Erden ist
[Observe that which
is above
and not that
which is on earth]
>
> (Cave Creek Lutheran
> Cemetery, Gillespie County)

Other epitaphs speak of the German work ethic and the professions:

> Hier nun ruhet
> der die Erde sechzig
> Jahre hat gepflüget[36]
> [Here now rests
> the one who plowed the earth
> for sixty years]
>
> > (1900, Freethinker, Comfort
> > Cemetery, Kendall County)

Ueber 40 Jahre wirkte er
im Weinberg des Herrn zu
Round Top und Umgegend
[Over 40 years he labored
in the Lord's vineyard
in Round Top and vicinity]
>
> (Lutheran pastor, 1902,
> Round Top, Fayette County)

Wie ein sanfter Schlum-
mer der die Müden
nach der Tagesarbeit
    überfällt,
So des Frommen Tod,
er schlaft in Frieden,
sanft hinüber in die
    Bessere Welt.
[Like a soft slumber-
er that overtakes the
tired ones after a day's
    work
So [is] death to the pious
He sleeps in peace,
quietly passing over into the
    Better World]
                (1901, Lutheran Cemetery,
                Round Top, Fayette County)

Max H. Reinbach Apotheker
[Max H. Reinbach, apothecary]
                (1896, Fredericksburg
                Catholic Cemetery,
                Gillespie County)

Conclusion

All in all, the Texas German graveyards, with their fine craftsmanship, internal geometrical order, venerable hex signs, and distinctive use of the German language, are perhaps the most thoroughly Teutonic places left in the state. Those who would learn about this immigrant people ought to visit their burial places first—and quickly, because the culture and crafts of the *Alten*, the "old ones," are rapidly disappearing. In the final chapter, attention is directed to the endangered legacy of Texas' traditional graveyards.

A Legacy
Squandered?

THE MESSAGE of Chapters 2 through 5 is
that a rich, endangered, and heretofore largely
ignored heritage of traditional art, craftsmanship, and customs survives in the rural and
small-town graveyards of Texas. Vividly reflecting the complex ethnic mosaic of the
state, this funerary culture-complex is rapidly
deteriorating (Fig. 6-1). As an all-pervading
popular culture rises to ascendance, changing
our life-styles and preferences, Texans are in
the process of squandering this priceless
legacy of a simpler age. Recently, at a cemetery in Athens in East Texas, a family plot,
carefully scraped, mounded, and decorated
with shells, was reportedly leveled and planted
to grass at the order of the perpetual-care
association. All shells were removed and discarded. The action greatly distressed the aged
woman who had previously kept the plot in
the traditional southern manner, but she was
helpless to prevent the alteration. One can
only imagine the emotions called forth in this
elderly person when decorations, deemed fitting and necessary by countless generations,
were removed against her will from the
graves of her son and husband.

The aggressive Texas climate and mindless
vandals also bring steady deterioration and
sudden destruction to traditional graveyards
(see box; Fig. 6-2). Reservoir and highway construction takes an additional toll. Along Interstate 30 in Northeast Texas, I once stopped
to inspect a pathetic little family graveyard
trapped between the highway and service
road. The small cluster of humble stones
seemed to huddle protectively together, as if

FIG. 6-1. The weather, possibly assisted by vandals,
has already begun to ravage this fine old limestone
German marker in the Catholic cemetery at Fredericksburg. Its cross, held in place for this picture,
had already toppled, and part of the epitaph is no
longer legible. Commemorating a member of the
pioneer Stein family, the locally made tombstone
displays typically German symbols and hex signs,
including the heart, *Urbogen*, and pentacle *Drudenfuss* (see Chap. 5). Photo by the author, 1977.

FIG. 6-2. Vandalism is clearly a problem at the old town cemetery in Salado, Bell County. The weathered sign at the bottom advertises "curbs poured & dates set in stones." Photo by the author, 1980.

FIG. 6-3. This humble wooden graveshed, in Little Hope Cemetery, Wood County, is literally on its last legs and will soon perish unless preservation efforts are made. Its deteriorated condition is symptomatic of the endangered status of material folk culture in the rural graveyards of Texas. Photo by the author, 1980.

awaiting the eventual, inevitable assault of an errant eighteen-wheeler.

The distraught woman at Athens and the ravaged small cemetery alongside the Interstate symbolize the fate of all traditional culture in Texas. An Old Testament prophet, if permitted to view this situation, might ascend the nearest high place and declare woe unto a people who so thoughtlessly discard, destroy, and desecrate the customs and artifacts of countless generations of ancestors. If only the protective curse and magic of the German *Drudenfuss*, Mexican *mal ojo*, or Afro-American graveyard voodoo could shield the old burial grounds from the excesses of the modern age.

Actually, the legacy housed in our graveyards has survived longer than we of the popular culture and cities had any right to expect. Rural Texans, resisting immense pressures to change and obeying age-old cults of piety, have doggedly perpetuated many venerable customs and lovingly preserved numerous valuable artifacts of funerary folk culture down to the present day. Some century-old tombstones, marking the graves of long-forgotten dead ones, still receive frequent care and maintenance. But the ranks of these protectors and practitioners are now thinned and aged. Soon the last of them will have joined their forebears in the same graveyards they have labored so hard to maintain. Then, truly, Texan folk culture will have made its last stand and the ways of the old ones will vanish (Fig. 6-3).

We cannot rescue folk culture intact. Not even nations with governmental policies of historical preservation and restoration far more enlightened than ours have been able to do that. But we are capable of saving many of its artifacts. Even countries as comparatively poor as Ireland have done so. Some of the few remaining Texas folk cemeteries—at places like Terlingua, Indian Creek, and Old D'Hanis—ought, if possible, to be taken under the protection of the state government or some private foundation, to be maintained in the traditional way. Plaster casts should be made of outstanding tombstones, such as the Kellner marker at New Braunfels, the Old

Bethel effigy stones, the Adams markers at Indian Creek, the Braetta Gothic monument at Norse, and the stonework of Joseph Rudinger at St. Dominic, in order that replicas could be molded to adorn local and state museums. Fragile, critically endangered specimens of wooden craftsmanship, including the Frelsburg curbs, the San Elizario crosses, and a sampling of gravesheds, should be brought indoors and replaced by replicas (Fig. 6-4). Some way must be found to preserve permanently the Herbort metal markers, the Oak Ridge lichgate, the Ysleta perforated nameplate, and other outstanding examples of German, Hispanic, and Anglo decorative ironwork.

We should undertake this preservation effort not just because a priceless legacy of beautiful traditional art and craftsmanship is endangered, but also because folk graveyards are such revealing and remarkable records of our several cultural heritages. By no means have we deciphered all the messages that the cemetery culture complex can pass on to us

"VANDALS DAMAGE MARKERS IN MOUNT GILEAD CEMETERY"

"KELLER [, Texas]—Vandals desecrated the old Mount Gilead Cemetery earlier this week, toppling over monuments and breaking headstones.

"Ed Grimes, president of the Mt. Gilead Cemetery Association who is cleaning up the old burial park, said he is not sure when the vandalism took place.

"The cemetery was intact when he finished work Friday, Grimes said, and when he returned Tuesday, 19 markers had been damaged.

"'Some of them were turned over and some were broken. It's just sick,' Mrs. Grimes said. . . .

"Sunday will be homecoming for the Mt. Gilead Baptist Church, located across the street from the cemetery, and Grimes said he is cleaning up the park for that event. . . .

"The nearby Bourland Cemetery also was vandalized about two years ago."

—Undated clipping from the *Fort Worth Star-Telegram*, 1975, in Peggy Gough, "The Upland Southern Cemetery Tradition in Tarrant County, Texas," graduate research paper.

FIG. 6-4. The wood weathered away less rapidly beneath a painted epitaph on this old German marker in the Lutheran cemetery at Quihi in Medina County, permitting the inscription to remain partially legible in bas relief for a few more years. It cannot, without care and restoration, survive the century. The birthplace of the deceased, the German province of Ostfriesland (East Frisia) is still discernible. Photo courtesy of Professor Francis E. Abernethy of Stephen F. Austin State University, Nacogdoches, Texas.

about our remote forebears. These special places are not merely repositories for our dead, but actually museums full of obvious and subtle reminders from our ancient past and distant, diverse ancestral homelands (Fig. 6-5).

There is cause for hope. The American bicentennial celebration in the middle 1970s, together with Alex Haley's *Roots*, sent hundreds of lay volunteers into the graveyards of Texas to copy names and dates from fading epitaphs. The resulting records were often subsequently published.[1] To be sure, the goal of this effort was genealogical, and the volunteers succeeded in preserving only one small aspect of the graveyard legacy—from my viewpoint, one of the less important aspects. We now need to enlarge upon the work of the bicentennial root-seekers and commence a far-reaching effort to save fragments of the material folk culture housed in those same cemeteries. And we should do it soon, lest we come too late and the spirits of those long-dead folk craftsmen, whose work we have squandered, grow restless and vengeful.

FIG. 6-5. A legacy in wooden folk art squandered. This typical West Texas Hispanic *cerquita*, at San Lorenzo cemetery in El Paso County, is all but gone, and the cross, literally covered with carved inscriptions, is obviously endangered. Photo by the author, 1980.

Notes

1. The Truth about Cemeteries

1. Terry G. Jordan, "Population Origin Groups in Rural Texas," *Annals, Association of American Geographers* 60 (1970): 404–405 plus folded map.

2. Fred Kniffen, "Necrogeography in the United States," *Geographical Review* 57 (1967): 426–427; Terry G. Jordan and Lester Rowntree, *The Human Mosaic: A Thematic Introduction to Cultural Geography*, pp. 217–218.

3. Frank W. Young, "Graveyards and Social Structure," *Rural Sociology* 25 (1960): 446–450.

4. Donald B. Ball, "Social Activities Associated with Two Rural Cemeteries in Coffee County, Tennessee," *Tennessee Folklore Society Bulletin* 41 (1975): 93–98.

5. Martha Stone, "Field Study of Cemeteries in Tyler County," graduate research paper.

6. Jack Ward Thomas and Ronald A. Dixon, "Cemetery Ecology," *Natural History* 82, no. 3 (March 1973): 62; Yi-fu Tuan, *Landscapes of Fear*, pp. 128, 209–210.

7. James Deetz, *In Small Things Forgotten: The Archeology of Early American Life*, p. 88.

8. Kniffen, "Necrogeography," p. 427.

9. John Michael Vlach, *The Afro-American Tradition in Decorative Arts*, p. 139.

10. John R. Stilgoe, "Folklore and Graveyard Design," *Landscape* 22, no. 3 (Summer 1978): 22.

11. See, for example, John D. Combes, "Ethnography, Archaeology and Burial Practices among Coastal South Carolina Blacks," *Conference on Historic Site Archaeology, Papers* 7 (1972): 52–61; and David H. Watters, "Gravestones and Historical Archaeology: A Review Essay," *Markers: The Annual Journal of the Association for Gravestone Studies* 1 (1979–1980): 174–179.

12. An exception is Norbert F. Riedl et al., *A Survey of Traditional Architecture and Related Material Folk Culture Patterns in the Normandy Reservoir, Coffee County, Tennessee*, chapter 9.

13. William Lynwood Montell, *Ghosts along the Cumberland: Deathlore in the Kentucky Foothills*; J. Mason Brewer, *Dog Ghosts and Other Texas Negro Folk Tales; The Word on the Brazos*, pp. 122–123; George R. Nielson, "Folklore of the German-Wends in Texas," in *Singers and Storytellers*, p. 255.

14. A few notable exceptions are Sara Clark, "The Decoration of Graves in Central Texas with Seashells," in *Diamond Bessie and the Shepherds*, pp. 33–43; Dorothy Jean Michael, "Grave Decoration," in *Backwoods to Border*, pp. 129–136; and Beulah M. D'Olive Price, "The Custom of Providing Shelters for Graves," *Mississippi Folklore Quarterly* 7, no. 1 (1973): 8–10.

15. Jordan and Rowntree, *Human Mosaic*, chapter 7, "The Geography of Folk Culture," pp. 225–261, biographical sketch of Kniffen, p. 237; Gene Wilhelm, "A Tribute to Dr. Fred B. Kniffen," *Pioneer America* 3, no. 2 (July 1971): 1–7.

16. John Leighly, "Berkeley: Drifting into Geography in the Twenties," *Annals, Association of American Geographers* 69 (1979): 4–9; James J. Parsons, "The Later Sauer Years," ibid. 69 (1979): 9–15.

17. Kniffen, "Necrogeography," pp. 426–427.

18. Ibid., p. 427.

19. Donald Gregory Jeane, "The Traditional Upland South Cemetery," *Landscape* 18, no. 2 (Spring-Summer 1969): 139–142; Milton Newton, Jr., "The Annual Round in the Upland South: The Synchronization of Man and Nature through Culture," *Pioneer America* 3, no. 2 (July 1971): 68.

20. David E. Sopher, *The Geography of Religions*.

21. This increased interest can be seen in the appearance of such publications as Chuen-yan David Lai, "A *Feng-Shui* Model as a Location Index," *Annals, Association of American Geographers* 64

(1974): 506–513; John D. Gay, *The Geography of Religion in England*; Richard V. Francaviglia, "The Cemetery as an Evolving Cultural Landscape," *Annals, Association of American Geographers* 61 (1971): 501–509; and James R. Shortridge, "Patterns of Religion in the United States," *Geographical Review* 66 (1976): 420–434; in addition to unpublished theses and dissertations, such as Mary Philpot, "In This Neglected Spot: The Rural Cemetery in British Columbia," M.A. thesis; and Gordon M. Riedesel, "The Cultural Geography of Rural Cemeteries: Saunders County, Nebraska," M.A. thesis. See also the abstracts by Jerry Eidem and James W. Darlington in *Great Plains-Rocky Mountain Geographical Journal* 8 (1979): 74.

22. Pierre Deffontaines, *Géographie et religions*, pp. 43–67, 178–196; Sopher, *Geography of Religions*, p. 32.

23. Don Yoder (ed.), *American Folklife*.

24. Terry G. Jordan, "The Religious Material Culture of North Texas," paper read at the national meeting of the American Studies Association, San Antonio, November 8, 1975; "Antecedents of the Texas Folk Cemetery," paper read at the annual meeting of the Pioneer America Society, Aurora, Ohio, September 30, 1977; "A Religious Geography of the Hill Country Germans of Texas," paper read at the Symposium on Ethnicity on the Great Plains, sponsored by the University of Nebraska Center for Great Plains Studies, Lincoln, April 7, 1978; "Forest Folk, Prairie Folk: Rural Religious Cultures in North Texas," *Southwestern Historical Quarterly* 80 (1976): 135–162; "'The Roses So Red and the Lilies So Fair': Southern Folk Cemeteries in Texas," *Southwestern Historical Quarterly* 83 (1980): 227–258.

2. The Southern Folk Cemetery in Texas

This chapter is a version of my article, "'The Roses So Red and the Lilies So Fair': Southern Folk Cemeteries in Texas," *Southwestern Historical Quarterly* 83 (1980): 227–258, used by permission of the Texas State Historical Association.

1. See Terry G. Jordan, "The Traditional Southern Rural Chapel in Texas," *Ecumene* 8 (1976): 6–17.

2. Jeane, "Upland South Cemetery," pp. 39–41, and his "The Upland South Cemetery: An American Type," *Journal of Popular Culture* 11 (1978): 895–903; Marguerite Serena Rogers, "Death and Burial Customs among American Plantation Negroes," M.A. thesis; and Jordan, "Forest Folk, Prairie Folk," pp. 153–158.

3. Michael, "Grave Decoration," pp. 129–136.

4. Fred A. Tarpley, "Southern Cemeteries: Neglected Archives for the Folklorist," *Southern Folklore Quarterly* 27 (1963): 329.

5. C. K. Meek, *The Northern Tribes of Nigeria*, II, 105, 121; R. S. Rattray, *The Tribes of the Ashanti Hinterland*, II, 352.

6. A. B. Ellis, *The Ewe-Speaking Peoples of the Slave Coast of West Africa*, p. 158; Rogers, "Death and Burial Customs," pp. 28, 52.

7. Theodore Albrecht, "Religious Material Culture in Watauga County, North Carolina," graduate research paper; Doug Swaim (ed.), *Carolina Dwelling: Towards Preservation of Place*, p. 250.

8. Stone, "Cemeteries in Tyler County"; Anita Pitchford, "Cultural Influences in Cass County: A Cemetery Survey," graduate research paper.

9. James Agee and Walker Evans, *Let Us Now Praise Famous Men*, p. 437.

10. Meek, *Northern Tribes of Nigeria*, II, 105, 120.

11. Rattray, *Tribes of the Ashanti Hinterland*, II, figs. 64 and 65 following p. 352; Jordan and Rowntree, *Human Mosaic*, p. 128.

12. Frederick Burgess, *English Churchyard Memorials*, p. 69.

13. Pitchford, "Cultural Influences in Cass County."

14. Otto A. Rothert, *A History of Muhlenberg County*, pp. 20, 131–132.

15. Newbell Niles Puckett, *Folk Beliefs of the Southern Negro*, pp. 104–106; Michael, "Grave Decoration," p. 130; Rogers, "Death and Burial Customs," p. 28; Ernest Ingersoll, "Decoration of Negro Graves," *Journal of American Folk-Lore* 5 (1892): 68–69; H. Carrington Bolton, "Decorating of Graves of Negroes in South Carolina," *Journal of American Folk-Lore* 4 (1891): 214; Vlach, *Afro-American Tradition*, p. 142; Georgia Writers' Project, Works Projects Administration, *Drums and Shadows: Survival Studies among the Georgia Coastal Negroes*, p. 117; and Roy Sieber, *African Furniture and Household Objects*, pp. 16, 17. Sieber illustrates a chief's grave in north-central Zaïre covered with pottery and other objects.

16. R. S. Rattray, *Religion and Art in Ashanti*, p. 161; idem, *Tribes of the Ashanti Hinterland*, II, 353; P. Amaury Talbot, *Tribes of the Niger Delta: Their Religions and Customs*, p. 236; Vlach, *Afro-American Tradition*, p. 141; Georgia Writers' Project, *Drums and Shadows*, p. 130.

17. David M. Robinson, *Excavations at Olynthus*, part XI, vol. II, p. 182.

18. E. Estyn Evans, *Irish Folk Ways*, pp. 289, 293.

19. Puckett, *Folk Beliefs*, p. 106; Michael, "Grave

Decoration," p. 132; Rogers, "Death and Burial Customs," p. 28; Agee and Evans, *Let Us Now Praise Famous Men*, p. 437; Robinson, *Excavations at Olynthus*, part XI, vol. II, pp. 194–195.

20. Paul Geiger et al., *Atlas der Schweizerischen Volkskunde*, vol. II, part 6, p. 507, in "Kommentar."

21. Michael, "Grave Decoration," p. 136; Robinson, *Excavations at Olynthus*, part XI, vol. II, pp. 196–201.

22. Clark, "Decoration of Graves," pp. 33–43; Wayland D. Hand (ed.) *Popular Beliefs and Superstitions from North Carolina*, p. 94; Rogers, "Death and Burial Customs," pp. 28–29; Michael, "Grave Decoration," pp. 133–134; Puckett, *Folk Beliefs*, p. 105; Combes, "Ethnography, Archaeology and Burial Practices," p. 56.

23. Jordan, "Forest Folk, Prairie Folk," p. 155; Pitchford, "Cultural Influences in Cass County"; Stone, "Cemeteries in Tyler County"; Lynette Schroeder, "Upland Southern Burial Traditions in Montague County, Texas," graduate research paper.

24. Meek, *Northern Tribes of Nigeria*, II, 122; Rattray, *Tribes of the Ashanti Hinterland*, II, 447–448; 463; Vlach, *Afro-American Tradition*, pp. 143–144; Sara Clark, "Grave Decoration in the Mexican-American Cemeteries of New Braunfels, Texas: Especially the Use of Sea Shells," manuscript, pp. 20, 36.

25. John R. Swanton, *The Indians of the Southeastern United States*, pp. 252–253, 728; William J. Perry, *The Children of the Sun*, p. 70; Eddie W. Wilson, "The Shell and the American Indian," *Southern Folklore Quarterly* 16 (1952):198.

26. E. O. James, *The Cult of the Mother-Goddess: An Archaeological and Documentary Study*, p. 16; Mircea Eliade, *Images and Symbols: Studies in Religious Symbolism*, p. 137; Clark, "Decoration of Graves," pp. 33–43.

27. Erich Neumann, *The Great Mother: An Analysis of the Archetype*; Grant Showerman, *The Great Mother of the Gods*; James, *Cult of the Mother-Goddess*, p. 129.

28. H. Cutner, *A Short History of Sex-Worship*, pp. 36, 39.

29. James, *Cult of the Mother-Goddess*, p. 149; Showerman, *Great Mother of the Gods*, pp. 273–274.

30. Cutner, *History of Sex-Worship*, pp. 37–38; Eliade, *Images and Symbols*, p. 125; Neumann, *The Great Mother*, p. 45.

31. Erwin Panofsky, *Tomb Sculpture*, plate 125; Ian Cox (ed.), *The Scallop: Studies of a Shell and Its Influence on Humankind*, pp. 34–48; Burgess, *English Churchyard Memorials*, pp. 73, 159–160; James, *Cult of the Mother-Goddess*, p. 43; Robinson, *Excavations at Olynthus*, part XI, vol. I, pp. 67, 94, 102, 198–199, and part V, vol. I, p. 125.

32. Eliade, *Images and Symbols*, p. 132; Burgess, *English Churchyard Memorials*, following p. 176.

33. Kenneth Lindley, *Of Graves and Epitaphs*, p. 100; Burgess, *English Churchyard Memorials*, pp. 183–184.

34. [Panola County Historical Commission], *A History of Panola County, Texas, 1819–1978*, p. 105.

35. Ball, "Social Activities," pp. 93–98; Jon McConal, "Cemetery Working: A Link with the Past," *Fort Worth Star Telegram*, July 16, 1977, p. 1b; Emma Guest Bourne, *A Pioneer Farmer's Daughter of Red River Valley, Northeast Texas*, p. 104; Darrell Debo, *Burnet County History: A Pioneer History, 1847–1979*, p. 142; and Georgia Writers' Project, *Drums and Shadows*, p. 147. The latter reference mentions the southern black custom of providing food for the dead at the wake.

36. Lucy Ames Edwards, "Stories in Stone: A Study of Duval County Grave Markers," *Florida Historical Quarterly* 35 (1956–1957):120.

37. Wilbur Zelinsky, "Unearthly Delights: Cemetery Names and the Map of the Changing American Afterworld," in *Geographies of the Mind: Essays in Historical Geosophy*, ed. David Lowenthal and Martyn J. Bowden, p. 181.

38. Pitchford, "Cultural Influences in Cass County."

39. Neumann, *The Great Mother*, pp. 261–262, plate 128b; Showerman, *Great Mother of the Gods*, p. 260.

40. Thomas Bodkin, *The Virgin and Child*, pp. 6–7; Ernst Guldan, *Eva und Maria: Eine Antithese als Bildmotiv*, frontispiece; Estelle M. Hurll, *The Madonna in Art*, pp. 113, 196; Neumann, *The Great Mother*, p. 326.

41. Enid Porter, *Cambridgeshire Customs and Folklore*, p. 30; Geiger et al., *Atlas der Schweizerischen Volkskunde*, vol. II, part 6, pp. 509–512, in "Kommentar."

42. Hurll, *Madonna in Art*, p. 196; Edith Hamilton, *Mythology*, p. 23.

43. Pitchford, "Cultural Influences in Cass County."

44. Showerman, *Great Mother of the Gods*, pp. 298, 300.

45. Schroeder, "Upland Southern Burial Traditions"; Charles L. Templeton, "Folk Cemeteries: A Grave Situation in Grayson County, Texas," graduate research paper; Peggy G. Gough, "The Upland Southern Cemetery Tradition in Tarrant County, Texas," graduate research paper; and Stone, "Cemeteries in Tyler County."

46. Jeane, "Upland South Cemetery," p. 41; Geiger et al., *Atlas der Schweizerischen Volkskunde*, vol. II, part 6, p. 512 in "Kommentar."

47. Zelinsky, "Unearthly Delights," p. 180.

48. Neumann, *The Great Mother*, pp. 50, 242.

49. Ibid., p. 245.

50. Vaughan Cornish, *The Churchyard Yew and Immortality.*

51. James, *Cult of the Mother-Goddess*, p. 134; Lindley, *Of Graves and Epitaphs*, p. 90.

52. Lindley, *Of Graves and Epitaphs*, p. 84.

53. Erwin Rohde, *Psyche: The Cult of Souls and Belief in Immortality among the Greeks*, pp. 141, 189.

54. Jeane, "Upland South Cemetery," p. 40; Puckett, *Folk Beliefs*, p. 94.

55. Jeane, "Upland South Cemetery," p. 40; Hand, *Popular Beliefs and Superstitions*, p. 91.

56. McConal, "Cemetery Working," p. 1b.

57. Burgess, *English Churchyard Memorials*, pp. 25–26, 53.

58. Stilgoe, "Folklore and Graveyard Design," p. 23.

59. Hand, *Popular Beliefs and Superstitions*, p. 91.

60. Rattray, *Religion and Art in Ashanti*, p. 162; idem, *Tribes of the Ashanti Hinterland*, I, 214, II, 535; personal communication from Professor John M. Vlach of the University of Texas at Austin, dated May 8, 1980.

61. John R. Swanton, *Indian Tribes of the Lower Mississippi Valley and Adjacent Coast of the Gulf of Mexico*, p. 325; idem, "Social Organization and Social Usages of the Indians of the Creek Confederacy," in *Forty-Second Annual Report of the Bureau of American Ethnology, 1924–1925*, p. 398.

62. Guldan, *Eva and Maria*, p. 253.

63. Jeane, "Upland South Cemetery," p. 40.

64. Rattray, *Religion and Art in Ashanti*, pp. 70, 161; ibid, *Tribes of the Ashanti Hinterland*, I, 292; Georgia Writers' Project, *Drums and Shadows*, p. 196.

65. Combes, "Ethnography, Archaeology and Burial Practices," p. 56; and Georgia Writers' Project, *Drums and Shadows*, p. 196.

66. Jordan, "Forest Folk, Prairie Folk," p. 156.

67. Frank Baker, *John Wesley and the Church of England*, p. 214.

68. Stone, "Cemeteries in Tyler County"; Schroeder, "Upland Southern Burial Traditions"; Templeton, "Grave Situation in Grayson County."

69. Pitchford, "Cultural Influences in Cass County," p. 5.

70. Donald B. Ball, "Observations on the Form and Function of Middle Tennessee Gravehouses,"

Tennessee Anthropologist 2 (Spring 1977): 29–62; Jack Corn, "Covered Graves," *Kentucky Folklore Record* 23, no. 1 (1977): 34–37; James E. Cobb, "Supplementary Information on Gravehouses in Tennessee," *Tennessee Anthropological Association Newsletter* 3, no. 6 (November–December 1978): 4–7; Price, "Providing Shelters for Graves," pp. 8–10.

71. Pitchford, "Cultural Influences in Cass County"; Stone, "Cemeteries in Tyler County."

72. Ball, "Middle Tennessee Gravehouses," pp. 54–55.

73. William Bosman, *A New and Accurate Description of the Coast of Guinea, Divided into the Gold, the Slave, and the Ivory Coasts*, p. 232.

74. Meek, *Northern Tribes of Nigeria*, II, 120; Wilfrid D. Hambly, *The Ovimbundu of Angola*, p. 271 and plate XLVII.

75. Talbot, *Tribes of the Niger Delta*, pp. 250, 255; Meek, *Northern Tribes of Nigeria*, II, 116, 117.

76. Ball, "Middle Tennessee Gravehouses," p. 30; Swanton, *Indians of the Southeastern United States*, plate 88; Swanton, "Social Organization and Social Uses," pp. 394–396; Erminie Wheeler Voegelin, *Mortuary Customs of the Shawnee and Other Eastern Tribes*, pp. 341, 345.

77. Swanton, *Indians of the Southeastern United States*, pp. 722, 729; idem, "Social Organization and Social Uses," pp. 395–397.

78. John R. Swanton, *Source Material for the Social and Ceremonial Life of the Choctaw Indians*, p. 183, 185.

79. James W. Tyner and Alice Tyner Timmons, *Our People and Where They Rest*, II, 9.

80. Arthur B. Cozzens, "A Cherokee Graveyard," *Pioneer America* 4, no. 1 (January 1972): 8.

81. Jordan, "Forest Folk, Prairie Folk," p. 155; Pitchford, "Cultural Influences in Cass County."

82. Burgess, *English Churchyard Memorials*, pp. 20–21, 23.

83. Ibid., p. 26.

84. Georgia Writers' Project, *Drums and Shadows*, pp. 160, 165.

3. Traditional Southern Grave Markers

1. Burgess, *English Churchyard Memorials*, pp. 60–61; and Yvonne J. Milspaw, "Plain Walls and Little Angels," *Pioneer America* 12 (1980): 83.

2. Donald B. Ball, "Wooden Gravemarkers: Neglected Items of Material Culture," *Tennessee Folklore Society Bulletin* 43 (1977): 167–185; Jeane, "Upland South Cemetery," p. 899.

3. Francis E. Abernethy (ed.), *Tales from the Big Thicket*, pp. 47–48.

4. Ball, "Wooden Gravemarkers," pp. 167–170; Agee and Evans, *Let Us Now Praise Famous Men*, pp. 435–437; Combes, "Ethnography, Archaeology and Burial Practices," pp. 57, 59, 60; Georgia Writers' Project, *Drums and Shadows*, p. 117 and plate XII.

5. Burgess, *English Churchyard Memorials*, pp. 27–28; Deetz, *In Small Things Forgotten*, p. 88.

6. Robert F. Yehl, "A Geographic Analysis of the Cemeteries of Forsyth County, North Carolina," M.A. thesis, p. 35; Jeane, "Upland South Cemetery," p. 899.

7. Rothert, *History of Muhlenberg County*, p. 132.

8. Georgia Writers' Project, *Drums and Shadows*, p. 117 and plate XII.

9. For comparison with other states, see Mary Helen Weldy and David L. Taylor, "Gone But Not Forgotten: The Life and Work of a Traditional Tombstone Carver," *Keystone Folklore* 21 (1976–1977): 14–33; Diana Combs, "Eighteenth-Century Gravestone Art in Georgia and South Carolina," Ph.D. diss.; Edwards, "Stories in Stone," pp. 116–129; Henriette M. Forbes, *Gravestones of Early New England and the Men Who Made Them: 1653–1800*.

10. Jeane, "Upland South Cemetery," p. 899.

11. For comparison with tombstone decoration in the Middle Atlantic states, see Phil R. Jack, "Gravestone Symbols of Western Pennsylvania," in *Two Penny Ballads and Four Dollar Whiskey*, pp. 165–173.

12. Burgess, *English Churchyard Memorials*, p. 35.

13. Lindley, *Of Graves and Epitaphs*, p. 99; Burgess, *English Churchyard Memorials*, pp. 48, 119, 168, 172; Betty Willsher and Doreen Hunter, *Stones: A Guide to Some Remarkable Eighteenth Century Gravestones*, pp. 30, 39.

14. James Deetz and Edwin S. Dethlefsen, "Death's Head, Cherub, Urn, and Willow," *Natural History* 76, no. 3 (March 1967): 28–37.

15. Burgess, *English Churchyard Memorials*, p. 190.

16. Stone, "Cemeteries in Tyler County."

17. Lindley, *Of Graves and Epitaphs*, p. 106; Burgess, *English Churchyard Memorials*, p. 180.

18. James, *Cult of the Mother-Goddess*, p. 33; Burgess, *English Churchyard Memorials*, p. 158; Lindley, *Of Graves and Epitaphs*, p. 102.

19. Hurll, *Madonna in Art*, p. 165.

20. Burgess, *English Churchyard Memorials*, p. 178.

21. Lindley, *Of Graves and Epitaphs*, p. 108.

22. Burgess, *English Churchyard Memorials*,
pp. 94, 163–164, 184; Blanche M. G. Linden, "The Willow Tree and Urn Motif," *Markers: The Annual Journal of the Association for Gravestone Studies* 1 (1979–1980): 149–156.

23. Harvey H. Fuson, *Ballads of the Kentucky Highlands*, p. 126.

24. Willsher and Hunter, *Stones*, pp. 44, 50.

25. J. D. B. De Bow (ed.), *Statistical View of the United States . . . Being a Compendium of the Seventh Census*, pp. 45, 52, 145.

26. Stone, "Cemeteries in Tyler County."

27. Ibid.

28. Jordan, "Forest Folk, Prairie Folk," p. 158.

29. Stone, "Cemeteries in Tyler County."

30. Tarpley, "Southern Cemeteries," p. 330; Jordan, "Forest Folk, Prairie Folk," p. 158.

31. Willsher and Hunter, *Stones*, pp. 58, 121, 122.

32. Barbara W. Tuchman, *A Distant Mirror: The Calamitous 14th Century*, p. 125; Terry G. Jordan, "The Texan Appalachia," *Annals, Association of American Geographers* 60 (1970): 419; J. Gordon Bryson, *Culture of the Shin Oak Ridge Folk*, pp. 163–164; Clara Stearns Scarbrough, *Land of Good Water: A Williamson County, Texas, History*, pp. 187–188; Mrs. James C. Killen and Mrs. R. L. Vance (eds.), *History of Lee County, Texas*, p. 448.

33. Lori Youngblood, "Epitaphs," *Loblolly* 3, no. 2 (Fall 1975): 55.

34. Ibid.

35. Ibid., p. 53.

36. Ibid.

37. Templeton, "Grave Situation in Grayson County."

38. J. B. Jackson, "The Vanishing Epitaph: From Monument to Place," *Landscape* 17, no. 2 (Winter 1967): 22–26.

4. The Mexican Graveyard in Texas

1. See the illustrations in Francis E. Abernethy (ed.), *Built in Texas*, p. 96; Jim Steely, "Tombstone Territory," *Texas Highways* 23, no. 3 (March 1976): 6; Eugene George, *Historic Architecture of Texas: The Falcón Reservoir*, following p. 88; and Robert H. Adams, "Markers Cut by Hand," *American West* 4, no. 3 (August 1967): 59–61.

2. Stilgoe, "Folklore and Graveyard Design," p. 27.

3. Dorothy Benrimo et al., *Camposantos: A Photographic Essay*, p. 2; George M. Foster, *Culture and Conquest: America's Spanish Heritage*, p. 149.

4. Benrimo, *Camposantos*, p. 6.

5. Foster, *Culture and Conquest*, p. 148.

6. Benrimo, *Camposantos*, p. 3 and plates 4, 39, 40, 42, 62.

7. Ibid., p. 3.

8. Dorothy S. Kendall and Carmen Perry, *Gentilz: Artist of the Old Southwest*, p. 67. Pauline A. Pinckney, *Painting in Texas: The Nineteenth Century*, p. 171.

9. Adams, "Markers Cut by Hand," p. 59; Stilgoe, "Folklore and Graveyard Design," p. 27.

10. Stilgoe, "Folklore and Graveyard Design," p. 27; Adams, "Markers Cut by Hand," p. 59; Foster, *Culture and Conquest*, p. 152.

11. Clark, "Grave Decoration in the Mexican-American Cemeteries," p. 2.

12. Benrimo, *Camposantos*, pp. 6–7.

13. Ibid., p. 1.

14. Ibid., p. 3.

15. Foster, *Culture and Conquest*, p. 152.

16. Ibid.

17. Benrimo, *Camposantos*, plates 2, 14, 28, 47–52.

18. Adams, "Markers Cut by Hand," p. 59; Foster, *Culture and Conquest*, p. 152.

19. Personal comunication from Peggy Tobin of Bandera, Texas, March 27, 1980.

20. Clark, "Grave Decoration in the Mexican-American Cemeteries," p. 2.

21. Ibid., p. 1.

22. Ibid., pp. 6–8.

23. Ibid., p. 7.

24. Adams, "Markers Cut by Hand," p. 61; Benrimo, *Camposantos*, plates 3, 28.

25. Tobin, letter, March 27, 1980.

26. Clark, "Grave Decoration in the Mexican-American Cemeteries," p. 2.

27. Adams, "Markers Cut by Hand," p. 61; Stilgoe, "Folklore and Graveyard Design," p. 27; Benrimo, *Camposantos*, plates 2, 22, 31, 50, 65.

28. Most of my information about shell decoration is derived from Clark, "Grave Decoration in the Mexican-American Cemeteries," pp. 3–23.

29. Michael, "Grave Decoration," pp. 133–134.

30. Clark, "Grave Decoration in the Mexican-American Cemeteries," pp. 4, 5, 6, 8, 18.

31. James A. Michener, *Iberia: Spanish Travels and Reflections*, pp. 720, 757, 782; Cox, *The Scallop*, pp. 51–68.

32. Clark, "Grave Decoration in the Mexican-American Cemeteries," p. 14.

33. Steely, "Tombstone Territory," p. 6.

5. The Texas German Graveyard

1. Terry G. Jordan, "The German Element in Texas: An Overview," *Rice University Studies* 63, no. 3 (Summer 1977): 1–11.

2. For a comparison, see Preston A. Barba, *Pennsylvania German Tombstones: A Study in Folk Art*.

3. Johannes Schweizer, *Kirchhof und Friedhof: Eine Darstellung der beiden Haupttypen europäischer Begrabnisstätten;* Günther Grundmann and Konrad Hahm, *Schlesien*, p. 23; see also Terry G. Jordan, "A Religious Geography of the Hill Country Germans of Texas," in *Ethnicity on the Great Plains*, p. 121.

4. Gilbert J. Jordan, *Yesterday in the Texas Hill Country*, p. 95; Gilbert J. Jordan and Terry G. Jordan, *Ernst and Lisette Jordan: German Pioneers in Texas*, pp. 32, 40, 41.

5. Abernethy, *Built in Texas*, p. 276; E. M. Schiwetz, *Buck Schiwetz' Texas*, p. 59.

6. Terry G. Jordan, *German Seed in Texas Soil: Immigrant Farmers in Nineteenth-Century Texas*, pp. 199–200; Bradley H. Baltensperger, "Agricultural Change among Nebraska Immigrants," in *Ethnicity on the Great Plains*, pp. 181, 187.

7. Oscar Haas, *History of New Braunfels and Comal County, Texas, 1844–1946*, p. 205.

8. Jordan, *Ernst and Lisette Jordan*, pp. 29, 121.

9. See the "Plan von Friedrichsburg, Vereins Colonie am Piedernales, Texas 1846," in Carl von Solms-Braunfels, *Texas, Geschildert in Beziehung auf seine geographischen, socialen und übrigen Verhältnisse mit besonderer Rücksicht auf die deutsche Colonisation.*

10. A story related to the author by Frank E. Jordan of Mason County.

11. Jordan, "Forest Folk, Prairie Folk," pp. 158, 160.

12. Anne A. Fox and Katherine Livingston, *Historical, Architectural and Archaeological Investigations at the Steiner-Schob Complex, Victoria County, Texas*, p. 9.

13. Barba, *Pennsylvania German Tombstones*, p. 128; Charles H. Dornbusch and John K. Heyl, *Pennsylvania German Barns*, p. 88; Grundmann and Hahm, *Schlesien*, p. 23.

14. Clark, "Decoration of Graves," p. 40.

15. Hurll, *Madonna in Art*, p. 197; James, *Cult of the Mother-Goddess*, p. 163; Neumann, *The Great Mother*, pp. 45, 262, 308, plate 153. I observed pomegranates at Hortontown (New Braunfels), Grapetown, Castell, Hilda, and Hedwigs Hill.

16. O. Schwindrazheim, *Deutsche Bauernkunst*, pp. 98, 234, 237; Grundmann and Hahm, *Schlesien*, p. 23. Greater ornateness also distinguishes Pennsylvania German markers; see Milspaw, "Plain Walls," p. 83.

17. Abernethy, *Built in Texas*, p. 50.

18. Three generations of Joseph Rudingers are listed in the 1860 census for D'Hanis. Most likely the stonecutter was the one born about 1797 in France and listed as a "laborer." His presumed son, born about 1830, is another possibility (MSS free population schedules, Eighth Census of the United States, 1860, Medina County, Texas, p. 24, dwellings no. 210 and 211). Germans in the eastern United States also made splendid stone markers; see Klaus Wust, *Folk Art in Stone: Southwest Virginia*; Francis Y. Duval and Ivan B. Rigby, "Openwork Memorials of North Carolina," *Markers: The Annual Journal of the Association for Gravestone Studies* 1 (1979–1980): 65, 68, 73; Milspaw, "Plain Walls," pp. 86, 87, 89–93; and Barba, *Pennsylvania German Tombstones*.

19. For some Midwestern examples, see Julaine Maynard, "Wisconsin's Wrought Iron Markers," *Markers: The Annual Journal of the Association for Gravestone Studies* 1 (1979–1980): 77–80.

20. Schwindrazheim, *Deutsche Bauernkunst*, p. 93; Barba, *Pennsylvania German Tombstones*, pp. 6–7, 10, 215; Duval and Rigby, "Openwork Memorials," pp. 62, 65–68, 71, 73.

21. Barba, *Pennsylvania German Tombstones*, pp. 10, 113; Schwindrazheim, *Deutsche Bauernkunst*, p. 93; Klaus Wust, *The Virginia Germans*, p. iv.

22. Barba, *Pennsylvania German Tombstones*, pp. 8–9, 108–109; Schwindrazheim, *Deutsche Bauernkunst*, p. 98.

23. Barba, *Pennsylvania German Tombstones*, p. 2.

24. Ibid., pp. 11, 49; Schwindrazheim, *Deutsche Bauernkunst*, p. 37; Duval and Rigby, "Openwork Memorials," p. 72.

25. Barba, *Pennsylvania German Tombstones*, pp. 125, 208.

26. Schwindrazheim, *Deutsche Bauernkunst*, pp. 95, 98, 237.

27. Johann Wolfgang von Goethe, *Faust und Urfaust*, pp. 53, 56.

28. Barba, *Pennsylvania German Tombstones*, p. 21; Duval and Rigby, "Openwork Memorials," p. 72.

29. Schwindrazheim, *Deutsche Bauernkunst*, p. 98.

30. Grundmann and Hahm, *Schlesien*, p. 23.

31. The only published collection of Texas German epitaphs, complete with verse translation, appears in Gilbert J. Jordan, *German Texana: A Bilingual Collection of Traditional Materials*, pp. 59–74.

32. I am assuming that the nonexistent word *Genicht* in the epitaph is intended to be *geneigt*, "inclined to" or "disposed to," rendered in the translation as "gladly." The corruption permits the German rhyme to be continued.

33. The word should be *schliesse*.

34. The reformed spelling instituted in Germany in the 1880s remained unknown to the Texas Germans, and they continued to spell words in the old way. *Berather* instead of *Berater* is an example.

35. Anglicized spelling of *Vaterland*.

36. The word order is incorrect.

6. A Legacy Squandered?

1. See, for example, *Bandera County Cemetery Records*, compiled for the County Historical Survey Committee by Mrs. Howard Denson, Mrs. Billy Burnes, and Mrs. Howard Graves, and its accompanying *Index, Bandera County Cemetery Book*, mimeographed.

Bibliography

Books and Articles

Abernethy, Francis E. (ed.). *Built in Texas*. Publications of the Texas Folklore Society, no. 42. Waco: E-Heart Press, 1979.

———. (ed.). *Tales from the Big Thicket*. Austin: University of Texas Press, 1966.

Adams, Robert H. "Markers Cut by Hand." *American West* 4, no. 3 (August 1967): 59–64.

Agee, James, and Walker Evans. *Let Us Now Praise Famous Men*. Boston: Houghton Mifflin Co., 1939.

Arthur, Eric, and Dudley Witney. *The Barn: A Vanishing Landmark in North America*. Toronto: M. F. Feheley Arts Co., 1972.

Baker, Frank. *John Wesley and the Church of England*. Nashville and New York: Abingdon Press, 1970.

Ball, Donald B. "Observations on the Form and Function of Middle Tennessee Gravehouses." *Tennessee Anthropologist* 2 (Spring 1977): 29–62.

———. "Social Activities Associated with Two Rural Cemeteries in Coffee County, Tennessee." *Tennessee Folklore Society Bulletin* 41 (1975): 93–98.

———. "Wooden Gravemarkers: Neglected Items of Material Culture." *Tennessee Folklore Society Bulletin* 43 (1977): 167–185.

Baltensperger, Bradley H. "Agricultural Change among Nebraska Immigrants." In *Ethnicity on the Great Plains*, ed. Frederick C. Luebke, pp. 170–189. Lincoln: University of Nebraska Press, 1980.

Barba, Preston A. *Pennsylvania German Tombstones: A Study in Folk Art*. Pennsylvania German Folklore Society Yearbook, 18 (1953). Allentown, Pa.: Schlechter's, 1954.

Benes, Peter. *The Masks of Orthodoxy: Folk Gravestone Carving in Plymouth County, Massachusetts, 1689–1805*. Amherst: University of Massachusetts Press, 1977.

Benrimo, Dorothy; Rebecca S. James; and E. Boyd. *Camposantos: A Photographic Essay*. Fort Worth: Amon Carter Museum of Western Art, 1966.

Bodkin, Thomas. *The Virgin and Child*. New York: Pitman Publishing Co., 1949.

Bolton, H. Carrington. "Decorating of Graves of Negroes in South Carolina." *Journal of American Folk-Lore* 4 (1891): 214.

Bosman, William. *A New and Accurate Description of the Coast of Guinea, Divided into the Gold, the Slave, and the Ivory Coasts*. London: James Knapton, 1705.

Bourne, Emma Guest. *A Pioneer Farmer's Daughter of Red River Valley, Northeast Texas*. Dallas: Story Book Press, 1950.

Brewer, J. Mason. *Dog Ghosts and Other Texas Negro Folk Tales / The Word on the Brazos: Negro Preacher Tales from the Brazos Bottoms of Texas*. Austin: University of Texas Press, 1976.

Bryson, J. Gordon. *Culture of the Shin Oak Ridge Folk*. Austin: Firm Foundation Publishing House, 1964.

Burgess, Frederick. *English Churchyard Memorials*. London: Lutterworth Press, 1963.

Clark, Sara. "The Decoration of Graves in Central Texas with Seashells." In *Diamond Bessie and the Shepherds*, pp. 33–43. Publications of the Texas Folklore Society, 36. Austin: Encino Press, 1972.

Cobb, James E. "Supplementary Information on Gravehouses in Tennessee." *Tennessee Anthropological Association Newsletter* 3, no. 6 (November–December 1978): 4–7.

Coleman, J. Winston, Jr. (ed.). *Kentucky: A Pictorial History*. Lexington: University Press of Kentucky, 1971.

Combes, John D. "Ethnography, Archaeology and Burial Practices among Coastal South Carolina Blacks." *Conference on Historic Site Archaeology, Papers* 7 (1972): 52–61.

Corn, Jack. "Covered Graves." *Kentucky Folklore Record* 23, no. 1 (1977): 34–37.

Cornish, Vaughan. *The Churchyard Yew and Immortality*. London: Frederick Muller, 1946.

Cox, Ian (ed.). *The Scallop: Studies of a Shell and Its Influence on Humankind*. London: Shell Transport & Trading Co., 1957.

Cozzens, Arthur B. "A Cherokee Graveyard." *Pioneer America* 4, no. 1 (January 1972): 8.

Cutner, H. *A Short History of Sex-Worship*. London: Watts & Co., 1940.

Darden, Joe T. "Factors in the Location of Pittsburgh's Cemeteries." *Virginia Geographer* 7, no. 2 (1972): 3–8.

Darlington, James W. "Consistency and Variation in Rural and Small-Town Cemetery Landscapes." [Abstract.] *Great Plains-Rocky Mountain Geographical Journal* 8 (December 1979): 74.

Debo, Darrell. *Burnet County History: A Pioneer History, 1847–1979*. Vol. 1. Burnet: Eakin Press, 1979.

De Bow, J. D. B. (ed.). *Statistical View of the United States . . . Being a Compendium of the Seventh Census*. Washington, D.C.: A. O. P. Nicholson, 1854.

Deetz, James. *In Small Things Forgotten: The Archeology of Early American Life*. Garden City, N.Y.: Anchor Press/Doubleday, 1977.

———, and Edwin S. Dethlefsen. "Death's Head, Cherub, Urn and Willow." *Natural History* 76, no. 3 (March 1967): 28–37.

Deffontaines, Pierre. *Géographie et religions*. Paris: Gallimard, 1948.

Denson, Mrs. Howard; Mrs. Billy Burnes; and Mrs. Howard Graves. *Bandera County Cemetery Records* and *Index, Bandera County Cemetery Book*. Mimeographed. Bandera, Tex.: Bandera County Historical Survey Committee, [ca. 1976].

Dornbusch, Charles H., and John K. Heyl. *Pennsylvania German Barns*. Pennsylvania German Folklore Society Yearbook, 21 (1956). Allentown, Pa.: Schlechter's, 1958.

Downs, Virginia. "Folk Poetry in Gravestone Verse." *Kentucky Folklore Record* 25, nos. 1–2 (January–June 1979): 28–36.

Duval, Francis Y., and Ivan B. Rigby. "Openwork Memorials of North Carolina." *Markers: The Annual Journal of the Association for Gravestone Studies* 1 (1979–1980): 62–75.

Edwards, Lucy Ames. "Stories in Stone: A Study of Duval County Grave Markers." *Florida Historical Quarterly* 35 (1956–1957): 116–129.

Eidem, Jerry. "Reflections of Life in the Cemetery of the Upper Midwest." [Abstract.] *Great Plains-Rocky Mountain Geographical Journal* 8 (December 1979): 74.

Eliade, Mircea. *Images and Symbols: Studies in Religious Symbolism*. Translated by Philip Mairet. New York: Sheed & Ward, 1969.

Ellis, A. B. *The Ewe-Speaking Peoples of the Slave Coast of West Africa*. Chicago: Benin Press, 1965.

Evans, E. Estyn. *Irish Folk Ways*. London: Routledge and Kegan Paul, 1957.

[Federal Writer's Project, Works Progress Administration]. *Mississippi: A Guide to the Magnolia State*. New York: Viking Press, 1938.

Fielder, George F., Jr.; Steven R. Ahler; and Benjamin Barrington. *Historic Sites Reconnaissance of the Oak Ridge Reservation, Oak Ridge, Tennessee*. Oak Ridge: Oak Ridge National Laboratory, 1977.

Forbes, Henriette M. *Gravestones of Early New England and the Men Who Made Them: 1653–1800*. Boston: Houghton Mifflin Co., 1927.

Foster, George M. *Culture and Conquest: America's Spanish Heritage*. New York: Wenner-Gren Foundation for Anthropological Research, 1960.

Fox, Anne A., and Katherine Livingston. *Historical, Architectural and Archaeological Investigations at the Steiner-Schob Complex, Victoria County, Texas*. Archaeological Survey Report 52, San Antonio, Center for Archaeological Research, The University of Texas at San Antonio, 1979.

Francaviglia, Richard V. "The Cemetery as an Evolving Cultural Landscape." *Annals, Association of American Geographers* 61 (1971): 501–509.

French, Stanley. "The Cemetery as Cultural Institution: The Establishment of Mount Auburn and the 'Rural Cemetery' Movement." In *Death in America*, ed. David E. Stannard, pp. 69–91. Philadelphia: University of Pennsylvania Press, 1975.

Fuson, Harvey H. *Ballads of the Kentucky Highlands*. London: Mitre Press, 1931.

Gay, John D. *The Geography of Religion in England*. London: Gerald Duckworth, 1971.

Geiger, Paul; Richard Weiss; Walter Escher; and Elsbeth Liebl. *Atlas der Schweizerischen Volkskunde*. Basel: Schweizerische Gesellschaft für Volkskunde, 1951–1973.

George, Eugene. *Historic Architecture of Texas: The Falcón Reservoir*. Austin: Texas Historical Commission and Texas Historical Foundation, 1975.

Georgia Writers' Project, Works Projects Administration. *Drums and Shadows: Survival Studies among the Georgia Coastal Negroes.* Athens: University of Georgia Press, 1940.

Goethe, Johann Wolfgang von. *Faust und Urfaust.* Leipzig: Dieterich'schen Verlagsbuchhandlung, 1940.

Grundmann, Günther, and Konrad Hahm. *Schlesien.* No. 8 in the series *Deutsche Volkskunst.* Munich: Delphin Verlag, [1926].

Guldan, Ernst. *Eva und Maria: Eine Antithese als Bildmotiv.* Graz and Cologne: Hermann Böhlaus, 1966.

Haas, Oscar. *History of New Braunfels and Comal County, Texas, 1844–1946.* Austin: Steck Co., 1968.

Hambly, Wilfrid D. *The Ovimbundu of Angola.* Field Museum of Natural History, Publication 329, Anthropological Series 21, no. 2. Chicago, 1934.

Hamilton, Edith. *Mythology.* Boston: Little, Brown & Co., 1940.

Hand, Wayland D. *Popular Beliefs and Superstitions from North Carolina.* VII of *The Frank C. Brown Collection of North Carolina Folklore,* ed. Newman Ivey White. Durham, N.C.: Duke University Press, 1964.

Hannon, Thomas J., Jr. "Nineteenth Century Cemeteries in Central-West Pennsylvania." *Proceedings of the Pioneer America Society* 2 (1973):23–38.

Haseltine, Maury. "A Progress Report on the Pictorial Documentation of Early Utah Gravestones." In *Forms upon the Frontier: Folklife and Folk Arts in the United States,* ed. Austin Fife, Alta Fife, and Henry H. Glassie, pp. 79–88. Logan: Utah State University Press, 1969.

Howett, Catherine. "Living Landscapes for the Dead." *Landscape* 21, no. 3 (Spring–Summer 1977):9–17.

Hurll, Estelle M. *The Madonna in Art.* Boston: L. C. Page & Co., 1897.

Ingersoll, Ernest. "Decoration of Negro Graves." *Journal of American Folk-Lore* 5 (1892):68–69.

Jack, Phil R. "Gravestone Symbols of Western Pennsylvania." In *Two Penny Ballads and Four Dollar Whiskey,* ed. Kenneth S. Goldstein and Robert H. Byington, pp. 165–173. Hatsboro: Folklore Associates for the Pennsylvania Folklore Society, 1966.

Jackson, J. B. "The Vanishing Epitaph: From Monument to Place." *Landscape* 17, no. 2 (Winter 1967):22–26.

James, E. O. *The Cult of the Mother-Goddess: An Archaeological and Documentary Study.* New York: Frederick A. Praeger, 1959.

Jeane, Donald Gregory. "A Plea for the End of Tombstone-Style Geography." *Annals, Association of American Geographers* 62 (1972): 146–148.

———. "The Traditional Upland South Cemetery." *Landscape* 18, no. 2 (Spring–Summer 1969): 139–142.

———. "The Upland South Cemetery: An American Type." *Journal of Popular Culture* 11 (1978):895–903.

Jordan, Gilbert J. *German Texana: A Bilingual Collection of Traditional Materials.* Burnet, Tex.: Eakin Press, 1980.

———. *Yesterday in the Texas Hill Country.* College Station: Texas A&M University Press, 1979.

———, and Terry G. Jordan. *Ernst and Lisette Jordan: German Pioneers in Texas.* Austin: Von Boeckmann-Jones Co., 1971.

Jordan, Terry G. "Forest Folk, Prairie Folk: Rural Religious Cultures in North Texas." *Southwestern Historical Quarterly* 80 (1976):135–162.

———. "The German Element in Texas: An Overview." *Rice University Studies* 63, no. 3 (Summer 1977):1–11.

———. *German Seed in Texas Soil: Immigrant Farmers in Nineteenth-Century Texas.* Austin: University of Texas Press, 1966.

———. "Population Origin Groups in Rural Texas." *Annals, Association of American Geographers* 60 (1970):404–405 and folded map.

———. "A Religious Geography of the Hill Country Germans of Texas." In *Ethnicity on the Great Plains,* ed. Frederick C. Luebke, pp. 109–128. Lincoln: University of Nebraska Press, 1980.

———. "'The Roses So Red and the Lilies So Fair': Southern Folk Cemeteries in Texas." *Southwestern Historical Quarterly* 83 (1979–1980): 227–258.

———. "The Texan Appalachia." *Annals, Association of American Geographers* 60 (1970): 409–427.

———. "The Traditional Southern Rural Chapel in Texas." *Ecumene* 8 (1976):6–17.

———, and Lester Rowntree. *The Human Mosaic: A Thematic Introduction to Cultural Geography.* 2d ed. New York: Harper & Row, 1979.

Kelke, William Hastings. *The Churchyard Manual, Intended Chiefly for Rural Districts.* London: C. Cox, 1851.

Kendall, Dorothy Steinbomer, and Carmen Perry. *Gentilz: Artist of the Old Southwest.* Austin: University of Texas Press, 1974.

Killen, Mrs. James C., and Mrs. R. L. Vance (eds.). *History of Lee County, Texas*. Quanah, Tex.: Nortex Press, for the Lee County Historical Survey Committee, 1974.

Kniffen, Fred. "Necrogeography in the United States." *Geographical Review* 57 (1967): 426–427.

Kull, Andrew. *New England Cemeteries: A Collector's Guide*. Brattleboro, Vt.: Stephen Greene Press, 1975.

Lai, Chuen-yan David. "A *Feng-Shui* Model as a Location Index." *Annals, Association of American Geographers* 64 (1974): 506–513.

Leighly, John. "Berkeley: Drifting into Geography in the Twenties." *Annals, Association of American Geographers* 69 (1979): 4–9.

Leighton, Betty. "Tabernacle at Vanderpool." *The Bandera County Historian* 2, no. 2 (Winter 1980): 2–3.

Letcher, Peter M. "The Breaks, Virginia." *Pioneer America* 4, no. 2 (July 1972): 1–7.

Linden, Blanche M. G. "The Willow Tree and Urn Motif." *Markers: The Annual Journal of the Association for Gravestone Studies* 1 (1979–1980): 149–156.

Lindley, Kenneth. *Of Graves and Epitaphs*. London: Hutchinson, 1965.

Ludwig, Allan I. *Graven Images: New England Stonecarving and Its Symbols, 1650–1815*. Middletown, Conn.: Wesleyan University Press, 1966.

Maynard, Julaine. "Wisconsin's Wrought Iron Markers." *Markers: The Annual Journal of the Association for Gravestone Studies* 1 (1979–1980): 77–80.

Meek, C. K. *The Northern Tribes of Nigeria*. 2 vols. London: Oxford University Press, 1925.

Michael, Dorothy Jean. "Grave Decoration." In *Backwoods to Border*, pp. 129–136. Publications of the Texas Folklore Society, 18. Dallas: Southern Methodist University Press, 1943.

Michener, James A. *Iberia: Spanish Travels and Reflections*. New York: Random House, 1968.

Milspaw, Yvonne J. "Plain Walls and Little Angels." *Pioneer America* 12 (1980): 76–96.

———. "Segregation in Life, Segregation in Death: Landscape of an Ethnic Cemetery." *Pennsylvania Folklife* 30, no. 1 (Autumn 1980): 36–40.

Montell, William Lynwood. *Ghosts along the Cumberland: Deathlore in the Kentucky Foothills*. Knoxville: University of Tennessee Press, 1975.

Neumann, Erich. *The Great Mother: An Analysis of the Archetype*. Translated by Ralph Manheim. London: Routledge & Kegan Paul, 1955.

Newton, Milton, Jr. "The Annual Round in the Upland South: The Synchronization of Man and Nature through Culture." *Pioneer America* 3, no. 2 (July 1971): 63–73.

Nielson, George R. "Folklore of the German-Wends in Texas." In *Singers and Storytellers*, pp. 244–259. Publications of the Texas Folklore Society, 30. Dallas: Southern Methodist University Press, 1961.

Nock, A. D. "Cremation and Burial in the Roman Empire." *Harvard Theological Review* 25 (1932): 331–341.

Osborne, Brian S. "The Cemeteries of the Midland District of Upper Canada: A Note on Mortality in a Frontier Society." *Pioneer America* 6, no. 1 (January 1974): 46–55.

Panofsky, Erwin. *Tomb Sculpture*. New York: H. N. Abrams, 1964.

[Panola County Historical Commission]. *A History of Panola County, Texas, 1819–1978*. N.p., 1979.

Parsons, James J. "The Later Sauer Years." *Annals, Association of American Geographers* 69 (1979): 9–15.

Pattison, William. "The Cemeteries of Chicago: A Phase of Land Utilization." *Annals, Association of American Geographers* 45 (1955): 245–257.

Perry, William J. *The Children of the Sun*. London: Methuen & Co., 1923.

Pinckney, Pauline A. *Painting in Texas: The Nineteenth Century*. Austin: University of Texas Press, 1967.

Porter, Enid. *Cambridgeshire Customs and Folklore*. New York: Barnes & Noble, 1969.

Price, Beulah M. D'Olive. "The Custom of Providing Shelters for Graves." *Mississippi Folklore Quarterly* 7, no. 1 (1973): 8–10.

Price, Larry W. "Some Results and Implications of a Cemetery Study." *Professional Geographer* 18 (1966): 201–207.

Puckett, Newbell Niles. *Folk Beliefs of the Southern Negro*. Chapel Hill: University of North Carolina Press, 1926.

Rattray, R. S. *Religion & Art in Ashanti*. Oxford: Clarendon Press, 1927.

———. *The Tribes of the Ashanti Hinterland*. 2 vols. Oxford: Clarendon Press, 1932.

Riedl, Norbert F.; Donald B. Ball; and Anthony P. Cavender. *A Survey of Traditional Architecture and Related Material Folk Culture Patterns in the Normandy Reservoir, Coffee County, Tennessee*. Department of Anthropology, University of Tennessee, Report of Investigations no. 17. Knoxville, 1976.

Roberts, Warren E. "Traditional Tools as Symbols: Some Examples from Indiana Tombstones." *Pioneer America* 12, no. 1 (1980): 54–63.

Robinson, David M. *Excavations at Olynthus.*
14 parts. Baltimore: Johns Hopkins Press, 1929–
1952. Part V, "Mosaics, Vases, and Lamps of
Olynthus," 1933; Part XI, "Necrolynthia, A Study
in Greek Burial Customs and Anthropology,"
1942.

Roemer, Ferdinand von. *Texas: Mit besonderer
Rücksicht auf deutsche Auswanderung und die
physischen Verhältnisse des Landes nach eigener
Beobachtung geschildert.* Bonn: Adolphus Mar-
cus, 1849.

Rohde, Erwin. *Psyche: The Cult of Souls and Belief
in Immortaility among the Greeks.* Translated by
W. B. Hillis. New York: Harcourt, Brace & Co.,
1925.

Rothert, Otto A. *A History of Muhlenberg County.*
Louisville, Ky.: John P. Morton & Co., 1913.

Scarbrough, Clara Stearns. *Land of Good Water: A
Williamson County, Texas, History.* Georgetown:
Williamson County Sun, 1973.

Schiwetz, E. M. *Buck Schiwetz' Texas: Drawings
and Paintings by E. M. Schiwetz.* Austin: University of Texas Press, 1960.

Schweizer, Johannes. *Kirchhof und Friedhof: Eine
Darstellung der beiden Haupttypen europäischer
Begrabnisstätten.* Linz: Oberösterreichischer
Landesverlag, 1956.

Schwindrazheim, O. *Deutsche Bauernkunst.* 2d ed.
Vienna and Leipzig: Deutscher Verlag für Jugend
& Volk, 1931.

Shortridge, James R. "Patterns of Religion in the
United States. *Geographical Review* 66 (1976):
420–434.

Showerman, Grant. *The Great Mother of the Gods.*
Bulletin of the University of Wisconsin, 43.
Madison, 1901.

Sieber, Roy. *African Furniture and Household Objects.* Bloomington: Indiana University Press, 1980.

Smith, Elmer L. *Early American Grave Stone Designs.* Lebanon, Pa.: Applied Arts Publishers,
1968.

Smith, James M. "Puritanism: Self-Image Forma-
tion through Gravestone Form, Style, and Symbols." *Daughters of the American Revolution
Magazine* 114, no. 4 (April 1980): 470–485, 569.

Solms-Braunfels, Carl von. *Texas, Geschildert in
Beziehung auf seine geographischen, socialen
und übrigen Verhältnisse mit besonderer
Rücksicht auf die deutsche Colonisation*
Frankfurt am Main: Johann David Sauerländer's
Verlag, 1846.

Sopher, David E. *The Geography of Religions.*
Englewood Cliffs, N.J.: Prentice-Hall, 1967.

Steely, Jim. "Tombstone Territory." *Texas Highways* 23, no. 3 (March 1976): 4–8.

Stilgoe, John R. "Folklore and Graveyard Design."
Landscape 22, no. 3 (Summer 1978): 22–28.

Swaim, Doug (ed.). *Carolina Dwelling: Towards
Preservation of Place, in Celebration of the
North Carolina Vernacular Landscape.* The Student Publication of the School of Design, University of North Carolina, 26. Raleigh, 1978.

Swanton, John R. *The Indians of the Southeastern
United States.* Smithsonian Institution, Bureau
of American Ethnology, Bulletin 137. Washington, D.C.: Government Printing Office, 1946.

———. *Indian Tribes of the Lower Mississippi Valley and Adjacent Coast of the Gulf of Mexico.*
Smithsonian Institution, Bureau of American
Ethnology, Bulletin 43. Washington, D.C.: Government Printing Office, 1911.

———. "Social Organization and Social Usages of
the Indians of the Creek Confederacy." In *Forty-
Second Annual Report of the Bureau of American Ethnology, 1924–1925*, pp. 23–472. Washington, D.C.: Government Printing Office, 1928.

———. *Source Material for the Social and Ceremonial Life of the Choctaw Indians.* Smithsonian Institution, Bureau of American Ethnology,
Bulletin 103. Washington, D.C.: Government
Printing Office, 1931.

Talbot, P. Amaury. *Tribes of the Niger Delta: Their
Religions and Customs.* London: Frank Cass &
Co., 1932.

Tarpley, Fred A. "Southern Cemeteries: Neglected
Archives for the Folklorist." *Southern Folklore
Quarterly* 27 (1963): 323–333.

Thomas, David H.; Stanley South; and Clark S.
Larsen. *Rich Man, Poor Men: Observations of
Three Antebellum Burials from the Georgia
Coast.* American Museum of Natural History,
Anthropological Papers, 54, part 3. New York:
1977.

Thomas, Jack Ward, and Ronald A. Dixon. "Cemetery Ecology." *Natural History* 82, no. 3 (March
1973): 60–67.

Tuan, Yi-fu. *Landscapes of Fear.* New York: Pan-
theon Books, 1979.

Tuchman, Barbara W. *A Distant Mirror: The Calamitous 14th Century.* New York: Alfred A.
Knopf, 1978.

Tyner, James W., and Alice Tyner Timmons. *Our
People and Where They Rest.* University of
Oklahoma American Indian Institute, II. Nor-
man, 1970.

Vlach, John Michael. "Graveyard Decoration." In
The Afro-American Tradition in Decorative Arts,
pp. 139–147. Cleveland: Cleveland Museum of
Art, 1978.

Voegelin, Erminie Wheeler. *Mortuary Customs of*

the Shawnee and Other Eastern Tribes. Indiana Historical Society, Prehistory Research Series, II, no. 4. Indianapolis, 1944.

Waring, Mary A. "Mortuary Customs and Beliefs of South Carolina Negroes." *Journal of American Folk-Lore* 7 (1894): 318.

Warner, W. Lloyd. *The Living and the Dead: A Study of the Symbolic Life of Americans.* New Haven: Yale University Press, 1959.

Watters, David H. "Gravestones and Historical Archaeology: A Review Essay." *Markers: The Annual Journal of the Association for Gravestone Studies* 1 (1979–1980): 174–179.

Weldy, Mary Helen, and David L. Taylor. "Gone But Not Forgotten: The Life and Work of a Traditional Tombstone Carver." *Keystone Folklore* 21 (1976–1977): 14–33.

Wilhelm, Gene. "A Tribute to Dr. Fred B. Kniffen." *Pioneer America* 3, no. 2 (July 1971): 1–7.

Willsher, Betty, and Doreen Hunter. *Stones: A Guide to Some Remarkable Eighteenth Century Gravestones.* New York: Taplinger Publishing Co., 1978.

Wilson, Eddie W. "The Shell and the American Indian." *Southern Folklore Quarterly* 16 (1952): 192–200.

Wust, Klaus. *Folk Art in Stone: Southwest Virginia.* Edinburg, Va.: Shenandoah History, 1970.

———. *The Virginia Germans.* Charlottesville: University Press of Virginia, 1969.

Yoder, Don (ed.). *American Folklife.* Austin: University of Texas Press, 1976.

Young, Frank W. "Graveyard and Social Structure." *Rural Sociology* 25 (1960): 446–450.

Youngblood, Lori. "Epitaphs." *Loblolly* [Gary High School, Gary, Texas] 3, no. 2 (Fall 1975): 50–57.

Zelinsky, Wilbur. "Unearthly Delights: Cemetery Names and the Map of the Changing American Afterworld." In *Geographies of the Mind: Essays in Historical Geosophy*, ed. David Lowenthal and Martyn J. Bowden, pp. 171–195. New York: Oxford University Press, 1976.

Newspapers

"Archway and Gate Erected at Cemetery." *Cotulla Record* (Cotulla, Tex.), July 5, 1979, p. 1.

"Long Mountain Cemetery Cleaning Sunday." *Mason County News* (Mason, Tex.), May 10, 1979, p. 6.

McConal, Jon. "Cemetery Working: A Link with the Past." *Fort Worth Star-Telegram*, July 16, 1977, p. 1b.

Northern Standard (Clarksville, Tex.), November 28, 1846, p. 2.

Theses, Dissertations, and Research Papers

Albrecht, Theodore. "Religious Material Culture in Watauga County, North Carolina." Graduate research paper, special materials, N.T.S.U. Willis Library, Denton, 1975.

Allcorn, Darla. "The Lonesome Dove Baptist Church and Cemetery." Graduate research paper, special materials, N.T.S.U. Willis Library, Denton, 1975.

Clark, Sara. "Grave Decoration in the Mexican-American Cemeteries of New Braunfels, Texas: Especially the Use of Sea Shells." Paper, xerox copy in possession of T.G.J.

Combs, Diana. "Eighteenth-Century Gravestone Art in Georgia and South Carolina." Ph.D. dissertation, Emory University, 1978.

Gerbers, Ronald W. "The Country Cemetery as Cultural Epitaph: The Case of Penns and Nittany Valleys, Pennsylvania." M.A. thesis, Pennsylvania State University, 1979.

Gough, Peggy G. "The Upland Southern Cemetery Tradition in Tarrant County, Texas." Graduate research paper, special materials, N.T.S.U. Willis Library, Denton, 1975.

Philpot, Mary. "In This Neglected Spot: The Rural Cemetery in British Columbia." M.A. thesis, University of British Columbia, 1976.

Pitchford, Anita. "Cultural Influences in Cass County: A Cemetery Survey." Graduate research paper, special materials, N.T.S.U. Willis Library, Denton, 1979.

Riedesel, Gordon M. "The Cultural Geography of Rural Cemeteries: Saunders County, Nebraska." M.A. thesis, University of Nebraska at Omaha, 1979.

Rogers, Marguerite Serena. "Death and Burial Customs among American Plantation Negroes." M.A. thesis, Atlanta University, 1941.

Schroeder, Lynette. "Upland Southern Burial Traditions in Montague County, Texas." Graduate research paper, special materials, N.T.S.U. Willis Library, Denton, 1974.

Stone, Martha. "Field Study of Cemeteries in Tyler County." Graduate research paper, special materials, N.T.S.U. Willis Library, Denton, 1975.

Templeton, Charles L. "Folk Cemeteries: A Grave Situation in Grayson County, Texas." Graduate research paper, special materials, N.T.S.U. Willis Library, Denton, 1976.

Yehl, Robert F. "A Geographic Analysis of the Cemeteries of Forsyth County, North Carolina." M.A. thesis, University of North Carolina, 1978.

Correspondence

Booth, Mrs. Tony. Paris, Texas. Letter and completed questionnaire to T. G. J., 1976.

Ericson, Carolyn. Nacogdoches, Texas. Completed questionnaire to T. G. J., 1977.

Hogg, Marie (Mrs. Jack). Gilmer, Texas. Completed questionnaire and letter to T. G. J., August 29, 1977.

Tobin, Peggy. Bandera, Texas. Completed questionnaire and letters to T. G. J., February, 1980; March 27, 1980; April 8, 1980; April 23, 1980; April 24, 1980.

Vlach, John M. University of Texas at Austin. Personal communication to T. G. J., May 8, 1980.

Manuscript Documents

United States Census. MSS free population schedules of the Eighth Census, 1860. Microfilm copies available at the Willis Library, North Texas State University, Denton.

Papers Read at Professional Meetings

Becker, Nickie. "Tombstone Territory." Paper read at the 84th annual meeting of the Texas Academy of Science, University of Texas, Austin, March 19–21, 1981.

Jordan, Terry G. "Antecedents of the Texas Folk Cemetery." Paper read at the annual meeting of the Pioneer America Society, Aurora, Ohio, September 30, 1977.

———. "A Religious Geography of the Hill Country Germans of Texas." Paper read at the Symposium on Ethnicity on the Great Plains, sponsored by the University of Nebraska Center for Great Plains Studies, Lincoln, April 7, 1978.

———. "The Religious Material Culture of North Texas." Paper read at the national meeting of the American Studies Association, San Antonio, November 8, 1975.

Kremenak, Beverly. "East Texas Cemeteries: The Significance to Rural Communities." Paper read at the fall meeting of the Southwestern Division, Association of American Geographers, North Texas State University, Denton, October 17, 1980.

Maxfield, Orland. "Boston Mountain Cemeteries: Epilogue of Settlement." Paper read at the spring meeting of the Southwestern Division, Association of American Geographers and the Southwestern Social Science Association, Dallas, March 27, 1981.

Index